KT-222-911

Country Cross-Stitch

Sharon Perna

Sterling Publishing Co., Inc.   New York

This book is dedicated to my mother, Edwannah Hopper Perna, whom I love and admire for her own special interests in nutrition, exercise, and foreign languages.

Library of Congress Cataloging-in-Publication Data
Perna, Sharon.
    Country cross-stitch / Sharon Perna.
        p.   cm.
    ISBN 0-8069-5768-9 (H)
    1.   Cross-stitch—Patterns. I.   Title.
TT778.C76P42   1991
746.44′3041—dc20

91-12845
CIP

10   9   8   7   6   5   4   3   2

First paperback edition published in 1992 by
Sterling Publishing Company, Inc.
387 Park Avenue South, New York, N.Y. 10016
© 1991 by Sharon Perna
Distributed in Canada by Sterling Publishing
% Canadian Manda Group, P.O. Box 920, Station U
Toronto, Ontario, Canada M8Z 5P9
Distributed in Great Britain and Europe by Cassell PLC
Villiers House, 41/47 Strand, London WC2N 5JE, England
Distributed in Australia by Capricorn Link Ltd.
P.O. Box 665, Lane Cove, NSW 2066
Manufactured in the United States of America
All rights reserved

Sterling ISBN 0-8069-5768-9 Trade
                0-8069-5769-7 Paper

Color Photography by Nancy Palubniak

CONTENTS

Color Sections follow pages 16 and 48.

Preface

For as long as I can remember, I have always enjoyed a trip to the country and being surrounded by beautiful animals, fruits, flowers, and vegetables. My parents and grandparents were all avid gardeners, and they were also interested in animals of all kinds. So with a number of enthusiastic relatives, I had lots of childhood opportunities to visit state fairs, farmer's markets, stockyards, zoos, and farms of all sizes. As an adult I still cannot resist looking in everyone's garden and petting and feeding all farm animals within my reach. Through the years these memories of America's rich and bountiful land have inspired me. Recently these fond remembrances provided the theme for this third cross-stitch book.

In *Country Cross-Stitch*, it was my purpose to create 40 original and useful projects for the home. In designing these decorative pieces, I wanted to accent the kitchen and the living, family, dining, bath, and bedrooms with variations on the country theme. I also wanted the designs to incorporate a wide variety of motifs, colors, thread counts, fabrics, and sewing abilities. So there are simple designs on traditional fabrics for those who are new to counted cross-stitch and more advanced patterns for those who are truly sewing enthusiasts.

If you are familiar with my first and second cross-stitch books, *Treasury of Cross-Stitch Samplers* and *Love & Friendship Samplers*, both published by Sterling, you will notice that this one is organized slightly differently. Projects are arranged in groups that indicate the degree of difficulty, and I have taken care to try to place the charts on the same or facing pages as the color keys. I have also done my best to see that charts that were too big for one page have been divided and positioned on opposite rather than front to back pages. And in the section of the book entitled "Projects," the lists of materials, starting, and finishing directions are presented in a better and easier-to-follow format. So with all of these improvements, you should have more time to enjoy and sew the most beautiful country cross-stitch projects ever.

——SHARON PERNA

MATERIALS AND TECHNIQUES

Materials

THE FABRICS

Cross-stitching is done on an evenweave fabric of cotton or linen. "Evenweave" means that the fabric is evenly woven so that it has the same number of threads to the inch in both directions of the cloth (horizontally and vertically). Just as the textile you will embroider has a natural woven grid made by the crossing of the threads, the charted graph you will work from also has a corresponding framework, which matches it perfectly.

Aida is a 100% cotton fabric available in white, ivory, solid colors, and in multicolor combinations. It is usually sold in pre-cut pieces or by the bolt. The count of this fabric, that is, the number of cross-stitches you can sew in a one-inch space, is either 6, 8, 11, 14, or 18 (Illus. 1). You should also understand that the fabric count can be expressed in several different ways, but the interpretation is always the same. For example, 6 Aida, Aida 6, 6-count Aida cloth, and 6/1" all mean that you can embroider 6 cross-stitches per inch on that particular fabric. If a project calls for a specific count, using another count only alters and distorts the appearance of the design.

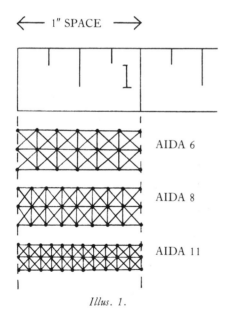

Illus. 1.

Linen is a cloth made from a very strong vegetable fibre called flax. Stitchers value it because it is an elegant, smooth, and durable fabric. Usually sold by the yard, linen comes in white (bleached), shades of ivory (natural or unbleached), and a few pastel colors. The most popular thread counts vary from 18 to 36 threads per inch. Since cross- and backstitches are stitched over two threads on linen, a thread count of, for example, 18 means you are actually making 9 cross-stitches per inch. It is also important to understand that as the thread count increases, the linen, obviously, becomes finer, tighter, and softer to the touch.

There are two things you need to learn about evenweave fabrics: The cotton or linen is never preshrunk; and the cloth frays easily. The first statement is a characteristic to accept. The fraying, however, can be managed in the following manner. Turn under ¼" on the raw edges of either the cotton or linen. Press this measurement towards the wrong side of the cloth. Then finish off the raw edges by either: Machine-stitching twice ⅛" from the edges (Illus. 2); whipping around the margins with a knotted double strand of thread (Illus. 3); or machine zigzag stitching twice around the piece (Illus. 4).

WRONG SIDE OF CLOTH

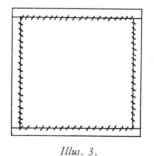

Illus. 2.

WRONG SIDE OF CLOTH

Illus. 3.

WRONG SIDE OF CLOTH

Illus. 4.

PERFORATED PAPER

As a needlecraft, perforated or punch-paper reached the height of its popularity in the late 19th century. Combined with either wool or silk floss, fashionable paper embroiderers stitched sentimental Valentines, bookmarks, colorful mottoes, and patriotic phrases for placement over doorways and fireplace mantels. They also incorporated such novel materials as beads and chenille into this delightful art form.

Perforated paper for needlework can be purchased in needlecraft, craft shops, and through the buyer's guide of many craft-oriented magazines. It is available in white or ivory and sold in sheets that measure 9″ × 12″ each.

Perforated paper has a thread count of 14. And like a 14-count Aida cloth, two strands of embroidery floss are used for cross- and backstitching. Because the holes in this lightweight cardboard are very pronounced, a threaded needle slips easily through as you embroider.

THREADS AND NEEDLES

In each cross-stitch key, two brands of six-ply cotton embroidery floss are given. The J. & P. Coats six-strand floss is listed first because that is what I use. Other embroiderers are die-hard DMC fans (their six-strand cotton is also referred to as mouliné spécial), so I have included their preference too. The final choice in the battle of the brands is up to you. Both products are excellent.

Embroidery floss is marketed in skeins of approximately nine yards each. You can use all six strands of the thread or separate it into one, two, or three strands cut into 14″ lengths. Since my artwork features perforated paper, cotton, and linen fabrics in a variety of counts, refer to the chart entitled "Using Evenweave Materials, Six-strand Cotton Embroidery Floss, and Needles in Combination." For this tells you the requirements for cross- or backstitching on different materials.

Tapestry needles have blunt points, and they vary in size from #13 (the largest and heaviest) to #26 (the smallest and lightest). For all the embroidery in this collection, use either a #24 or #26 needle as indicated in the previously mentioned chart.

Using Evenweave Materials, Six-strand Cotton Embroidery Floss, and Needles in Combination

Type of evenweave material	Strands of floss needed to cross-stitch	Strands of floss needed to backstitch	Size of tapestry needle	Sewing Instructions
Aida 8 (100% cotton)	3	2	24	Embroider one cross- or backstitch within one square on these evenweave materials.
Aida 11 (100% cotton)	2	2	24	
Aida 14 (100% cotton including Background Aida and Hopscotch or cotton blends including Fiddler's Cloth)	2	2	24 or 26	
Maxi-weave Ribband, 14-count (90% polyester and 10% cotton)	2	2	24 or 26	
Perforated paper, 14 count	2	2	24 or 26	
Aida 18 (100% cotton)	1	1	24 or 26	
Irish linen, 18-thread count	3	2	24	Embroider one cross- or backstitch over *two* threads on these evenweave fabrics.
Cork linen, 19-thread count	3	2	24	

MISCELLANEOUS SUPPLIES

When you have an evenweave material, some embroidery floss, scissors, and a tapestry needle, you really have all the essentials for cross-stitching. However, the following supplies are also useful:

Thimble.
Threads. For general sewing use cotton-covered (wrapped) polyester.
Rulers. A 12″ C-Thru is especially helpful.
Embroidery Hoops. Hoops are not necessary, but adjustable tambour frames are fine.
Tracing Paper. Sold in pads or in rolls, the light- and medium-weights are good for pattern-making.

100% Polyester Batting. Poly-fil traditional needle-punched batting is available in seamless sheets. It adds body to the embroidered surface, cuts like fabric, and is washable.
Dressmaker's Tracing Paper (Washable and Dry Cleanable). Dressmaker's tracing paper is used to transfer pattern markings to either the right or wrong side of a fabric. Although each packet contains an assortment of coated colored papers, use white whenever possible. The white markings disappear easily from either the heat of an iron or from washing. For light- and medium-colored fabrics, select the lightest possible color of dressmaker's tracing paper.

To mark a fabric always place the waxy side of the paper next to the cloth that is to be inscribed. Then lightly trace over the markings in the pattern with a sewing gadget called a tracing wheel (Illus. 5).

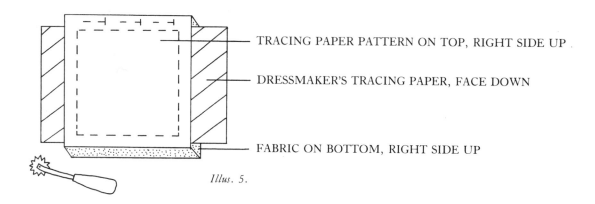

TRACING PAPER PATTERN ON TOP, RIGHT SIDE UP

DRESSMAKER'S TRACING PAPER, FACE DOWN

FABRIC ON BOTTOM, RIGHT SIDE UP

Illus. 5.

Stitching Techniques

All the designs in this book are made with cross-stitches alone or cross-stitches in combination with backstitches. Both stitches are simple to make and easy to master.

CROSS-STITCHING ON COTTON, LINEN, AND PERFORATED PAPER

Cross-stitches are worked by passing a blunt tapestry needle through the holes in a gridlike fabric. A completed cross-stitch is made in two movements: A left-to-right bottom stitch, which slants like this / and a right-to-left topstitch, which slants like this \ . The cross-stitches that result can be

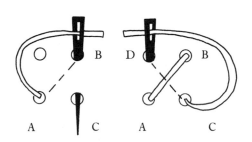

Illus. 6. Single cross-stitch.

a. Bring needle up through hole in fabric at lower left corner of cross (A). Insert thread diagonally across at hole B and come up at C. Pull thread through.

b. Complete other half of cross; stitch from C to D.

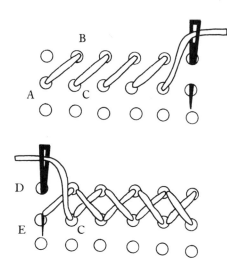

Illus. 7. Rows of cross-stitches.

a. Work first strokes left to right. Bring needle up through hole in fabric at A. Insert thread diagonally across at B and come up at C. Pull thread through. Continue to end of row.

b. On return journey, complete other half of cross sewing right to left. From C go over to D, then under and up to E (same hole as A).

made singly (Illus. 6) or embroidered in rows where the understitches are made in one direction, and the returns are worked in the opposite manner (Illus. 7). Cross-stitches can also be sewn in horizontal, vertical, and diagonal directions. The rules are: All the stitches must be crossed in the same direction; you make one cross-stitch within one square on an evenweave cotton or perforated paper (Illus. 8), and; you embroider one cross-stitch over *two* threads on linen (Illus. 9).

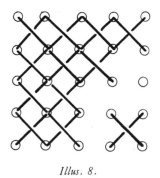

Illus. 8.

Illus. 9.

BACKSTITCHING ON COTTON, LINEN, AND PERFORATED PAPER

Backstitches (Illus. 10) add detail to a surface that is predominantly filled with cross-stitches. Since they are used as accents, backstitches are done after all the cross-stitching is complete. Like cross-stitches they can also be sewn horizontally, vertically, diagonally, or in line combinations. On an evenweave cotton or perforated paper, sew one backstitch within one square, but on linen remember to work over the two required threads (Illus. 11). On my charts, backstitches are indicated by bold black lines, and they are diagrammed in the direction they are to be embroidered.

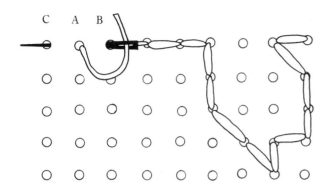 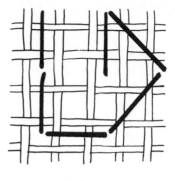

Illus. 11.

Illus. 10. Backstitches.

a. All stitches are same size.

b. Work right to left even though stitches travel in different directions.

c. Bring needle up through hole in fabric at A.

d. Take small running stitch backward to B and bring needle up in front of first stitch at C. Pull thread through.

e. Repeat taking another stitch backwards; put needle in same hole as A.

Basic Procedures

UNDERSTANDING THE CHARTS

Cross-stitch designs are not printed on fabrics. You recreate the embroidery by counting from a graph or chart. As you would expect, the graphs vary in their complexity and the degree of work they require.

As you look at each chart and work on the evenweave cotton or perforated paper, one square on the graph represents one square on the cotton or perforated paper that could be filled with one complete cross-stitch. For work on linen, one square on the graph also equals one cross-stitch, but the cross-stitch is embroidered over *two* threads on linen. The different symbols in the design represent where a cross-stitch should be made and which floss color needs to be used. Backstitches are indicated by bold black lines, and they are diagrammed in the direction they are to be sewn. Plain squares are areas that contain no embroidery.

MAKING THE FIRST CROSS-STITCH

In the "Projects," you will repeatedly see the heading "Making the first cross-stitch." Very specific instructions follow this phrase. For example, "Measure across 3¼″ from top left corner; measure downwards 4″ from top left corner. Mark the point where the two measurements intersect (Illus. 12). Start sewing at arrow." If you follow these directions, you will usually make your first cross-stitch at a temporarily marked spot on the fabric or paper, which corresponds to an arrow, which is almost always in the top left corner of the graph (Illus. 13). Refer to the cross-stitch key, and select the proper color of floss. Then continue by making all the cross-stitches to the right and by sewing the rest of the design from left-to-right and from top to bottom.

STARTING A THREAD

After you have cut and separated your floss into the proper number of strands, do not knot the ends. Leave, instead, a 1″ tail of floss hanging against the back of the material. Make

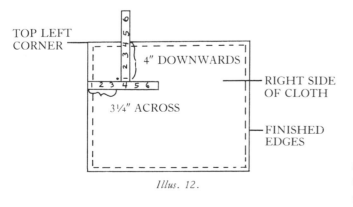

Illus. 12.

TOP LEFT CORNER

4″ DOWNWARDS

3¼″ ACROSS

RIGHT SIDE OF CLOTH

FINISHED EDGES

TOP LEFT CORNER OF GRAPH

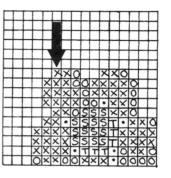

Illus. 13.

your first cross-stitches as you simultaneously secure the tail by working over it with the next few stitches (Illus. 14).

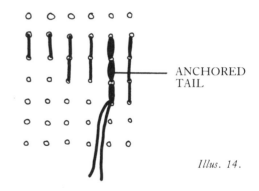

ANCHORED TAIL

Illus. 14.

ENDING A THREAD

To end a thread run your needle under four or five stitches on the back of the design and clip off the excess floss. Remember that the reverse side of the material should appear as neat as the front. Therefore, no hanging threads.

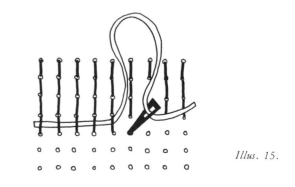

Illus. 15.

To begin a new thread after you have already worked several rows of embroidery, run your needle under four or five previously worked stitches on the reverse side of the material (Illus. 15). Then come up on the right side, and cross-stitch as usual.

CARRYING THREADS

You do not have to finish off your embroidery floss when one color ends, if it reappears in an adjacent area, and if the thread can be run under previous stitches. If, for example, you are making a yellow squash and the color reintroduces itself 1″ away in a basket, do not end the color in the first position. Instead, carry the floss to an out-of-the-way place, come up on the right side of the material, take one running stitch, and then let the thread dangle until it is needed again (Illus. 16). At that point in time, rethread it, duck under the previous stitches on the wrong side of the material, and travel to the new location. Continue sewing as usual. The one exception to this principle involves wide-open spaces. Try to avoid carrying a thread across an opening of ⅝″ or more.

Loose unsupported threads can show through the front of an article, and they detract from the beauty of the embroidery.

WASHING AND IRONING TECHNIQUES

Once the needlework is done, the fabric needs to be hand- or machine-washed before you proceed to the "Finishing directions." Even if the embroidery appears clean, launder it anyway. This may be the last time the piece is ever cleaned, and washing gives the fabric a nice neat look. To do this, use lukewarm water and a gentle soap.

With the iron set on cotton or linen, press the embroidery on both sides. Then lay the article flat until it has thoroughly dried.

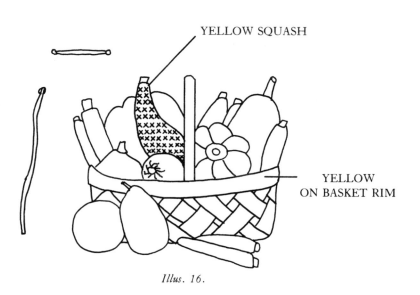

YELLOW SQUASH

YELLOW
ON BASKET RIM

Illus. 16.

The Cross-Stitch Summary (or How to Do a Project from Start to Finish)

Many of the cross-stitch procedures are repetitive, so I will list this information only once. I am now assuming, therefore, that you are completing this basic project routine, unless stated otherwise.

1. Choose a chart according to your sewing abilities. Within the "Project" section of the book, each project is grouped in categories of simple, intermediate, advanced or challenging.

2. All the materials and the details for "Making the first cross-stitch" are presented in the "Projects."

3. Do not preshrink evenweave cottons or linens. Do, however, preshrink any of the cottons which will be used as linings, backings, or trims.

4. Cut your evenweave materials to the exact measurements given. Seam allowances are included within these dimensions. Evenweave fabrics fray. Finish off the raw edges by either hand- or machine-stitching (Illus. 2-4).

5. In the upper left corner of the fabric or perforated paper, find the starting point for the first cross-stitch (Illus. 12). On the charted design this same reference point will be marked by an arrow (Illus. 13), which means start sewing here.

6. Do the embroidery by referring to the graph and cross-stitch key. All the cross-stitch keys list two brands of six-strand floss. You are to choose the floss from *either* the entire J. & P. Coats column on the left *or* the entire DMC column on the right. Thread your needle with the correct number of strands to be used for cross- and backstitching on your particular material. See the reference chart on page 9. For work on cotton and perforated paper, remember that one square on the graph represents one square on a material that can be filled with one complete cross-stitch. For work on linen, one square on the graph also equals one cross-stitch, but the cross-stitch is embroidered over *two* threads on linen. Backstitches are indicated by bold black lines, and they are diagrammed in the direction they are to be sewn. Sew the cross-stitches first; add the backstitches later.

7. Wash the completed embroidery. Press. Dry.

8. Consult the "Finishing directions."

9. Make all patterns that are required with tracing paper, pencil, and ruler.

10. To transfer any pattern markings to the right or wrong side of a fabric, always use the lightest possible color (white is preferable) of dressmaker's tracing paper and a tracing wheel (Illus. 5).

11. In the diagrams which accompany the "Finishing directions," a (R) means that the fabric is right side up; a (W) means the fabric is wrong side up.

Above: "Onions, Squashes, and Pumpkin," page 94. Left: "Potted Flowers," page 46.

A

Above: "Hunting Dogs," page 20.
Right: "Painted Basket," page 76.

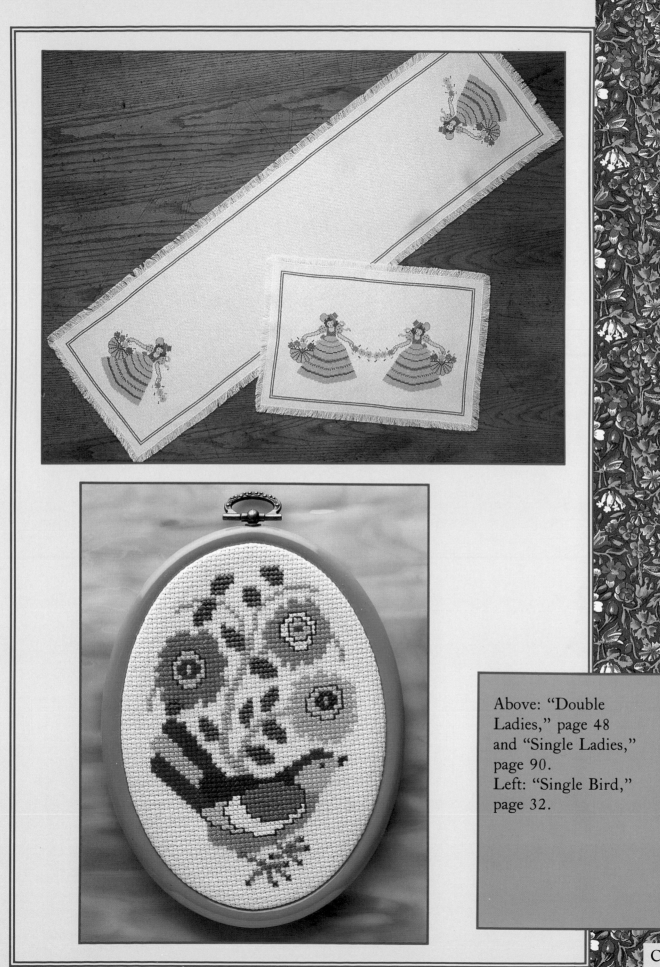

Above: "Double Ladies," page 48 and "Single Ladies," page 90.
Left: "Single Bird," page 32.

C

Above: "Purple Flowers," page 18. Right: "Bugs," page 22.

Above: "Barnyard Round-Up #1-3," page 62.
Left: "Spotted Dogs #1-4," page 42.

E

Above: "Growing
and Cut Flowers,"
page 92.
Right: "Horses,"
page 88.

Above: "Red Flow-
ers and Yellow
Birds," page 34.
Left: "Fruit Bas-
ket," page 100.

Above: "Cow and Calf," page 44 and "Weather Vanes," page 28.
Right: "Come Live with Me," page 111.

Come live with me, and be my love, and we will all the pleasures prove that valleys, groves, hills, and fields, woods or steepy mountain yields.

SIMPLE
PROJECTS

Purple Flowers *(In color, page D, Color Section I).*

Size: Bookmark approximately 2¼″ wide × 8″.

Perforated paper, 14-count, ivory: Cut paper 4¼″ wide × 9¾″.

Embroidery floss: Coats 6228 Christmas Green (or DMC 909), 6238 Chartreuse Bright (704), 3046 Christmas Red Bright (666), 5471 Coffee Brown (801), 4104 Lavender Dk. (210), 2302 Orange Lt. (743), 4101 Violet Dk. (552), and 4097 Violet Lt. (554). Purchase one skein of each.

Making the first cross-stitch: Measure across 1″ from top left corner; measure downwards ⅞″ from top left corner. Mark point where two measurements intersect. Start sewing at arrow.

Finishing directions
1. Do embroidery.
2. With right sides up, measure ¼″ beyond all four sides of design. Lightly pencil in these margins. Cut paper on lines.

CROSS-STITCH COLOR KEY

Symbol	J. & P. Coats	DMC
⊠	6228 Christmas Green	909
⊙	6238 Chartreuse Bright	704
·	3046 Christmas Red Bright	666
S	5471 Coffee Brown	801
△	4104 Lavender Dk.	210
╱	2302 Orange Lt.	743
e	4101 Violet Dk.	552
◆	4097 Violet Lt.	554
☐	Paper as is	

BACKSTITCH COLOR KEY

Symbol	Area	J. & P. Coats	DMC
	Details inside central flower and basket.	3046 Christmas Red Bright	666
	Outline around central flower.	4101 Violet Dk.	552

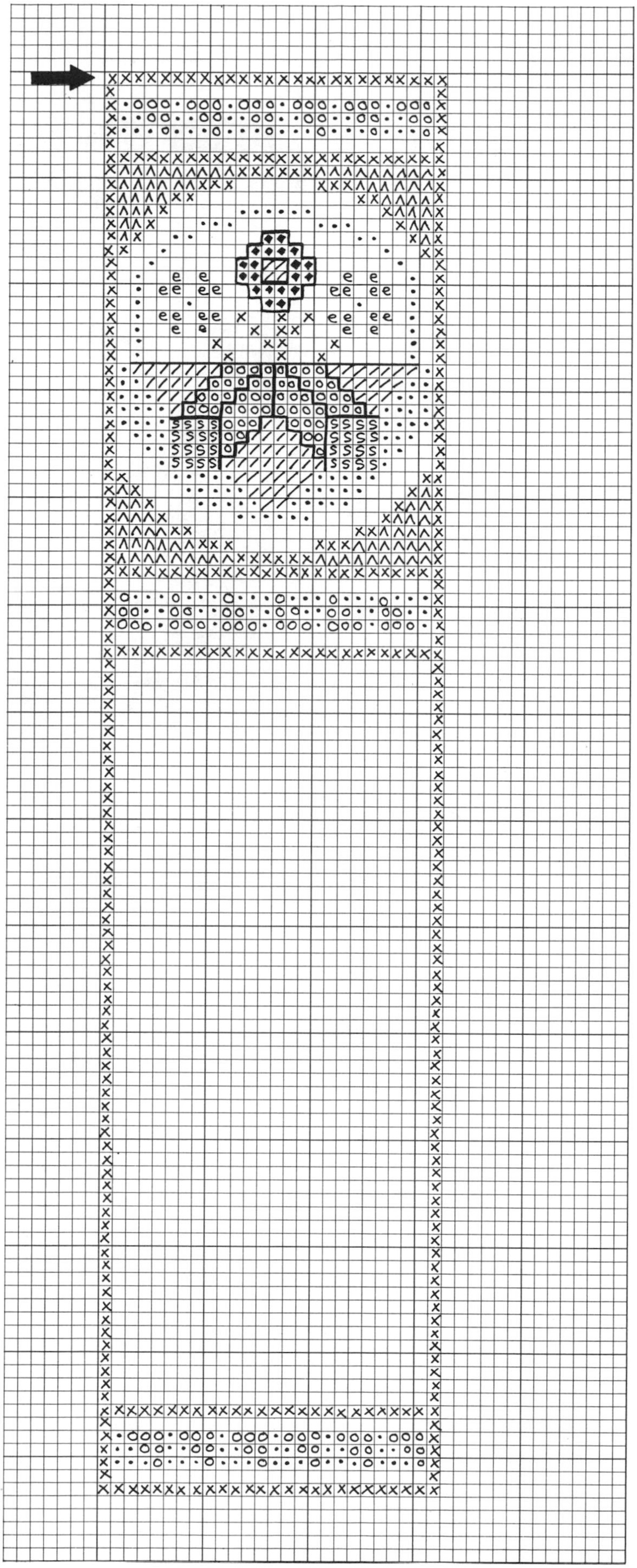

Hunting Dogs *(In color, page B, Color Section I).*

Size: Rectangle approximately 2¾″ wide × 2³⁄₁₆″.

Aida 18, ivory: Cut fabric 5½″ wide × 5″.

Embroidery floss: Coats 2326 Copper (or DMC 921), 8403 Black (310), 5471 Coffee Brown (433), 6258 Willow Green (987), 5363 Old Gold Lt. (676), and 5371 Topaz Very Ultra Dk. (use Coats color). Purchase one skein of each.

Other materials: Unbleached muslin, for backing, 5½″ wide × 5″. Stitch Witchery, 5½″ wide × 5″. White mat board, 3″ square. Two magnetic bars, ¼″ wide × ⅞″. Braided black nylon cording, ³⁄₃₂″ in diameter × 14″. White glue.

Making the first cross-stitch: Measure across 1¾″ from top left corner; measure downwards 1¾″ from top left corner. Mark point where two measurements intersect. Start sewing at arrow.

Finishing directions

1. Bond Aida to muslin with Stitch Witchery. With right sides up, place muslin flat, add Stitch Witchery, and position embroidery on top. Line up edges. Follow Stitch Witchery directions for bonding. Test for adhesion. Let fabric cool.
2. Count three blank squares of Aida beyond all four sides of embroidery. Mark with pins. Cut off excess fabric by following one row in Aida (Illus. 17).
3. Cut mat board the same size as Aida combination.
4. With right sides up, glue Aida combination to mat board. Spread glue across entire surface of board. Let dry.

5. Glue black cording to edges of Aida/mat board. Start in middle of bottom; complete by butting ends together. As the glue dries, keep pressing cording onto board.
6. Glue two magnetic bars to back of mat board (Illus. 18). Put weight on top. Let dry.

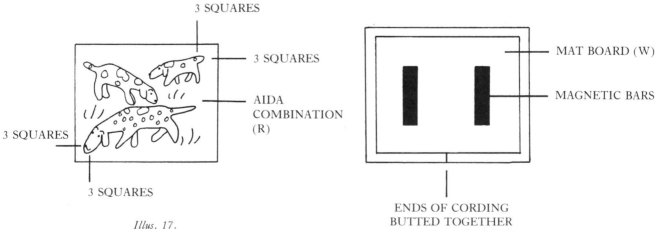

Illus. 17.

3 SQUARES

3 SQUARES

AIDA COMBINATION (R)

3 SQUARES

3 SQUARES

MAT BOARD (W)

MAGNETIC BARS

ENDS OF CORDING BUTTED TOGETHER

Illus. 18.

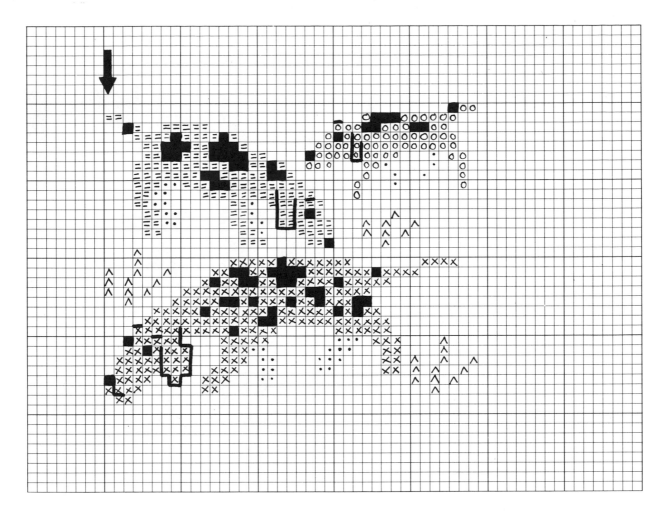

CROSS-STITCH COLOR KEY

Symbol	J. & P. Coats	DMC
⊠	2326 Copper	921
■	8403 Black	310
·	5471 Coffee Brown	433
△	6258 Willow Green	987
=	5363 Old Gold Lt.	676
⊙	5371 Topaz Very Ultra Dk.	Use J. & P. Coats color
□	Fabric as is	

BACKSTITCH COLOR KEY

Symbol	Area	J. & P. Coats	DMC
	All.	8403 Black	310

Bugs *(In color, page D, Color Section I)*.

Size: Aida inset approximately 2¾″ in diameter.

Aida 18, ivory: Premade fly swatter cover (burgundy cotton print with 2¾″ circular design area, outer dimensions 4½″ wide × 6½″ without edging (Illus. 19 and 20).

Embroidery floss: Coats 3021 Christmas Red Dk. (or DMC 498), 2326 Copper (921), 5363 Old Gold Lt. (use Coats color), 6267 Avocado Green (469), 6266 Apple Green (use Coats color), 5470 no name (434), 6228 Christmas Green (699), 8403 Black (310), 4092 Violet Med. (208), and 6239 Parrot Green Dk. (905). Purchase one skein of each.

Making the first cross-stitch: See Steps 1 and 2. Start sewing at arrow.

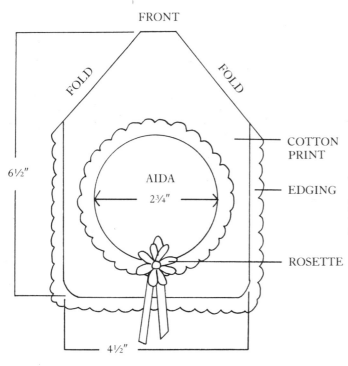

Illus. 19.

The rosette at the bottom of the inset takes up eight squares. Allow one blank square above rosette. Mark cloth with pins. Block off the area to be embroidered. Using knotted single strand of thread, hand-stitch edges of design by following

Finishing directions

1. Since your Aida inset may differ in size from mine, count horizontal and vertical squares at widest part of your circle. This design is 43 stitches wide and 37 stitches high. Subtract required squares from your figures. Divide the unusued squares by two. Arrange these numbers as margins (mine were four squares on left and top and three squares on right).

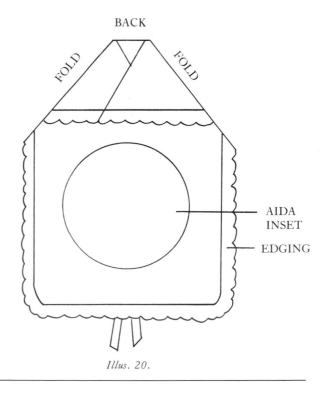

Illus. 20.

one row in Aida and by weaving in and out cloth with ½″ running stitches (Illus. 21). Refer to chart. Do embroidery.

2. If you do not have a rosette at the bottom of inset, these margins are suggested (Illus. 22).

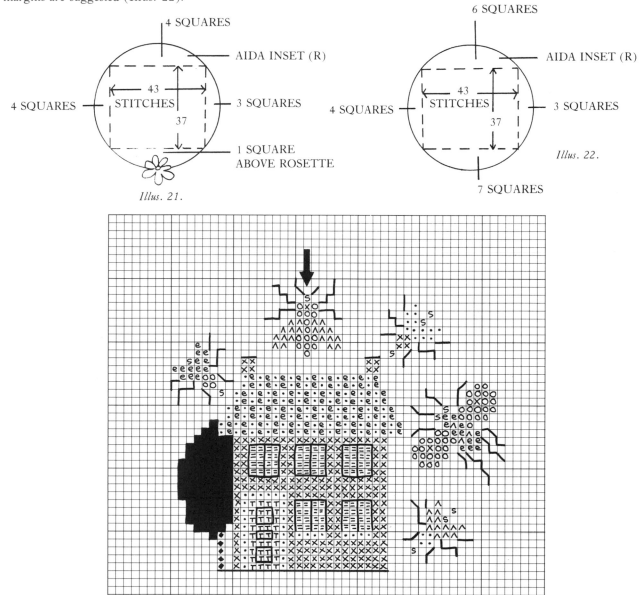

Illus. 21.

Illus. 22.

CROSS-STITCH COLOR KEY

Symbol	J. & P. Coats	DMC
·	3021 Christmas Red Dk.	498
e	2326 Copper	921
⊠	5363 Old Gold Lt.	Use J. & P. Coats color
=	6267 Avocado Green	469
T	6266 Apple Green	Use J. & P. Coats color
◆	5470 no name	434
■	6228 Christmas Green	699
S	8403 Black	310
o	4092 Violet Med.	208
∧	6239 Parrot Green Dk.	905
☐	Fabric as is	

BACKSTITCH COLOR KEY

Symbol	Area	J. & P. Coats	DMC
	Details on bugs.	8403 Black	310
	Chimney tops, lines around and within each window, and front door details.	3021 Christmas Red Dk.	498
	Vertical line beneath tree trunk and house.	6228 Christmas Green	699

Quilter's Motif

Size: Lid approximately 6″ wide × 4½″.

Perforated paper, 14-count, ivory: Cut paper 7″ wide × 5½″.

Embroidery floss: Coats 8403 Black (or DMC 310), 2290 Canary Bright (444), 4092 Violet Med. (552), 2300 Burnt Orange (741), 3046 Christmas Red Bright (666), 6238 Chartreuse Bright (704), and 6228 Christmas Green (909). Purchase one skein of each.

Other materials: Recipe file by Sudberry House (hinged, woodstain with 5″ wide × 3½″ design area, outer dimensions 6″ wide × 4½″, style #99081). Braided black nylon cording, ³⁄₃₂″ in diameter × ⅝ yard. White mat board, 6″ wide × 4½″. White glue.

Making the first cross-stitch: Measure across 1¼″ from top left corner; measure downwards 1¼″ from top left corner. Mark point where two measurements intersect. Start sewing at arrow.

Finishing directions

1. Cut mat board to precisely fit inside recessed area on lid (approximately 5″ wide × 3½″). With right sides up, glue board in lid.

2. Cut perforated paper to precisely fit inside recessed lid. To do, add ⅜″ margins beyond embroidery on sides. Add ¼″ margins beyond embroidery to top and bottom (Illus.

23). Check these measurements before your paper is cut.

3. With right sides up, glue perforated paper to top of mat board/lid. Apply glue to wrong side just on edges of paper. Let dry.

4. Glue black cording over edges of perforated paper/mat board/lid. Start in middle of bottom; complete by butting ends together (Illus. 24).

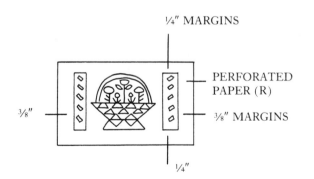

¼″ MARGINS

PERFORATED PAPER (R)

⅜″ MARGINS

⅜″

¼″

Illus. 23.

TOP VIEW OF LID

PERFORATED PAPER

WOOD

ENDS OF CORDING BUTTED TOGETHER

Illus. 24.

CROSS-STITCH COLOR KEY

Symbol	J. & P. Coats	DMC
⊡	8403 Black	310
·	2290 Canary Bright	444
△	4092 Violet Med.	552
T	2300 Burnt Orange	741
⊠	3046 Christmas Red Bright	666
⊟	6238 Chartreuse Bright	704
╱	6228 Christmas Green	909
☐	Paper as is	

BACKSTITCH COLOR KEY

Symbol	Area	J. & P. Coats	DMC
	Outer edge of both vertical bands.	3046 Christmas Red Bright	666
	Edge of purple flower.	4092 Violet Med.	552

Duck Decoys

Size: Rectangle approximately 2¹⁵⁄₁₆″ wide × 2″.

Aida 14, white: Cut fabric 6″ wide × 5″.

Embroidery floss: Coats 7159 Blue Very Lt. (or DMC 827), 5000 Russet (435), 3046 Christmas Red Bright (666), 5388 Beige (644), 6211 Jade Very Dk. (991), 2307 Christmas Gold (783), 3011 Coral (352), 5471 Coffee Brown (801), and 8403 Black (310). Purchase one skein of each.

Other materials: White Mini Tote by Hartin International (Illus. 25). White cotton, for backing, 6″ wide × 5″. Stitch Witchery, 6″ wide × 5″. Red soutache braid, 19″. White glue.

Making the first cross-stitch: Measure across 1½″ from top left corner; measure downwards 1½″ from top left corner. Mark point where two measurements intersect. Start sewing at arrow.

Finishing directions

1. Bond Aida to white cotton with Stitch Witchery. With right sides up, place cotton flat, add Stitch Witchery, and position embroidery on top. Line up edges. Follow Stitch Witchery directions for bonding. Test for adhesion. Let fabric cool.

2. Add margin of two blank squares of Aida to each side of embroidered design. Mark with pins. Cut off excess fabric by following one row in Aida.

3. Glue 3046 Christmas Red Bright Floss (use all six strands) to edges of rectangular design. Start in middle of bottom, and overlap ends by ½″. As glue dries keep pressing floss onto edges of fabric (Illus. 26).

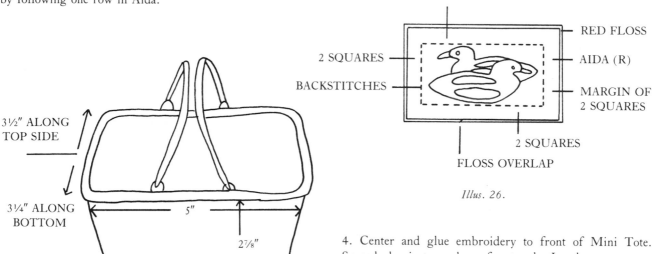

Illus. 26.

4. Center and glue embroidery to front of Mini Tote. Spread glue just on edges of rectangle. Let dry.

5. Glue soutache to top rim of tote. Start in middle of back; complete by butting ends together.

Illus. 25.

3½″ ALONG TOP SIDE

3¼″ ALONG BOTTOM

5″

4½″

2⅞″

2 SQUARES

RED FLOSS

2 SQUARES

AIDA (R)

BACKSTITCHES

MARGIN OF 2 SQUARES

2 SQUARES

FLOSS OVERLAP

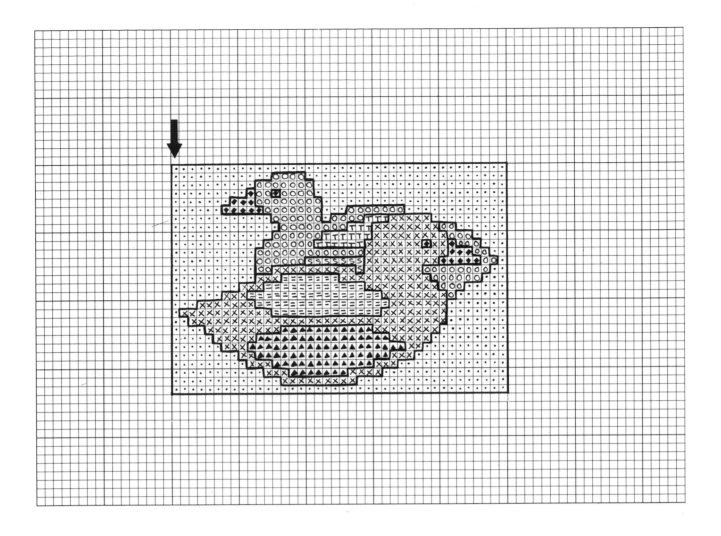

CROSS-STITCH COLOR KEY

Symbol	J. & P. Coats	DMC
·	7159 *Blue Very Lt.*	827
○	5000 *Russet*	435
◆	3046 *Christmas Red Bright*	666
T	5388 *Beige*	644
⊠	6211 *Jade Very Dk.*	991
=	2307 *Christmas Gold*	783
S	3011 *Coral*	352
▲	5471 *Coffee Brown*	801
☐	*Fabric as is*	

BACKSTITCH COLOR KEY

Symbol	Area	J. & P. Coats	DMC
	Outline around and within each decoy.	8403 *Black*	310
	Outline around rectangular shape.	3046 *Christmas Red Bright*	666

Weather Vanes *(In color, page H, Color Section I).*

Size: Aida inset approximately 5″ wide at top, 6″ wide at bottom, 2¾″ high on left, and 3⁷⁄₁₆″ high on right (Illus. 27).

Aida 14, white: Blue premade oven mitt by Ray Mar (The Country Manor Collection).

Embroidery floss: Coats 7030 Blue (or DMC 798), 7981 Navy Blue (use Coats color), 2300 Burnt Orange (741), 2326 Copper (921), 6256 Parrot Green Med. (906), and 7023 Blue Med. (796). Purchase one skein of each.

Making the first cross-stitch: See Steps 1 and 2. Start sewing at arrow.

Finishing directions

1. Mitt and chart are intentionally turned upside down to make this awkward sewing easier.
2. To make sure design fits on your mitt, block off the area to be embroidered. Design is 63 stitches wide and 41 stitches high. Try leaving ½″ margin on left. Mark cloth with pin. Count 63 stitches to right. Mark end with pin. Leave one blank square of Aida at top of design. Mark cloth with pin. Count 41 stitches to bottom. Mark end with pin. Using knotted single strand of thread, hand-stitch edges of design by following one row in Aida and by weaving in and out cloth with ½″ running stitches (Illus. 28).
3. Check also that top curve on largest rooster's tail fits in slanted Aida edge.

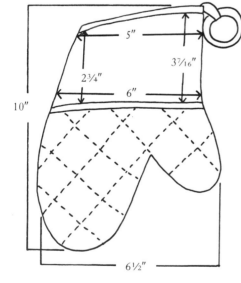

Illus. 27.

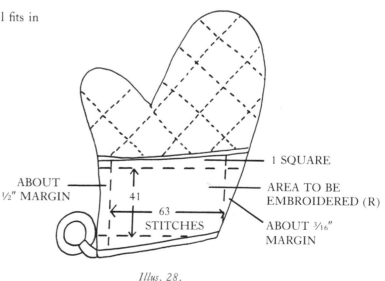

Illus. 28.

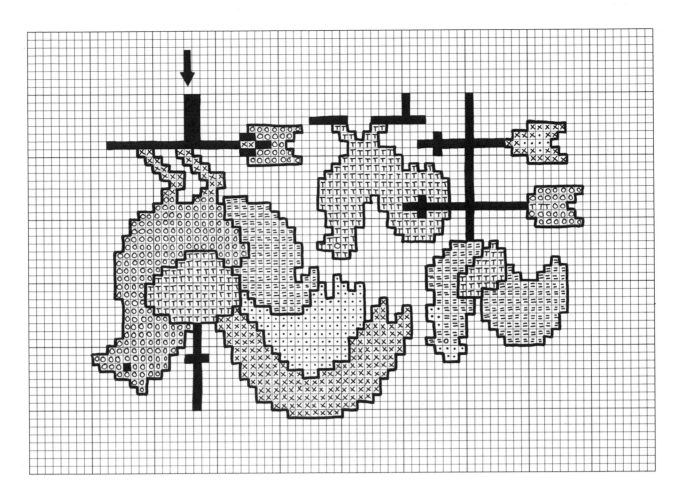

CROSS-STITCH COLOR KEY

Symbol	J. & P. Coats	DMC
⊠	7030 Blue	798
■	7981 Navy Blue	Use J. & P. Coats color
▣	2300 Burnt Orange	741
·	2326 Copper	921
T	6256 Parrot Green Med.	906
=	7023 Blue Med.	796
☐	Fabric as is	

BACKSTITCH COLOR KEY

Symbol	Area	J. & P. Coats	DMC
	All.	7981 Navy Blue	Use J. & P. Coats color

Tossed Design

Size: Lid approximately 9½″ wide × 3¾″.

Perforated paper, 14-count, ivory: Cut paper 10″ wide × 4¼″.

Embroidery floss: Coats 7981 Navy Blue (or DMC 336), 3001 Cranberry Lt. (899), 5470 no name (433), 7080 no name (798), 2302 Orange Lt. (743), 5371 Topaz Very Ultra Dk. (436), 6226 Kelly Green (702), and 3500 Christmas Red (321). Purchase one skein of each.

Other materials: Pencil box by Reed Baxter Woodcrafts (woodstain with 8⅛″ wide × 2½″ design area, outer dimensions 9½″ wide × 3¾″). White mat board, 10″ wide × 4¼″. Six small wire nails, ½ × 19 flat head.

Making the first cross-stitch: Measure across 1″ from top left corner; measure downwards 1″ from top left corner. Mark point where two measurements intersect. Start sewing at arrow.

Finishing directions
1. Remove particle board from design area.
2. Cut mat board to precisely fit inside entire lid (approximately 8¾″ wide × 3″).
3. With design centered, cut perforated paper same size as mat board.

4. Assemble box lid. With right sides down, place box lid flat, add perforated paper, mat board, and particle board. To permanently hold everything in position, gently hammer three nails on each long side of box (Illus. 29).

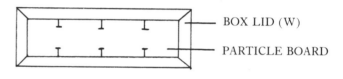

BOX LID (W)

PARTICLE BOARD

Illus. 29.

CROSS-STITCH COLOR KEY

Symbol	J. & P. Coats	DMC
⊠	7981 Navy Blue	336
·	3001 Cranberry Lt.	899
◻	5470 no name	433
T	7080 no name	798
△	2302 Orange Lt.	743
╱	5371 Topaz Very Ultra Dk.	436
=	6226 Kelly Green	702
■	3500 Christmas Red	321
☐	Paper as is	

BACKSTITCH COLOR KEY

Symbol	Area	J. & P. Coats	DMC
	All flower stems. Outline around yellow areas of basket.	6226 Kelly Green 7080 no name	702 798

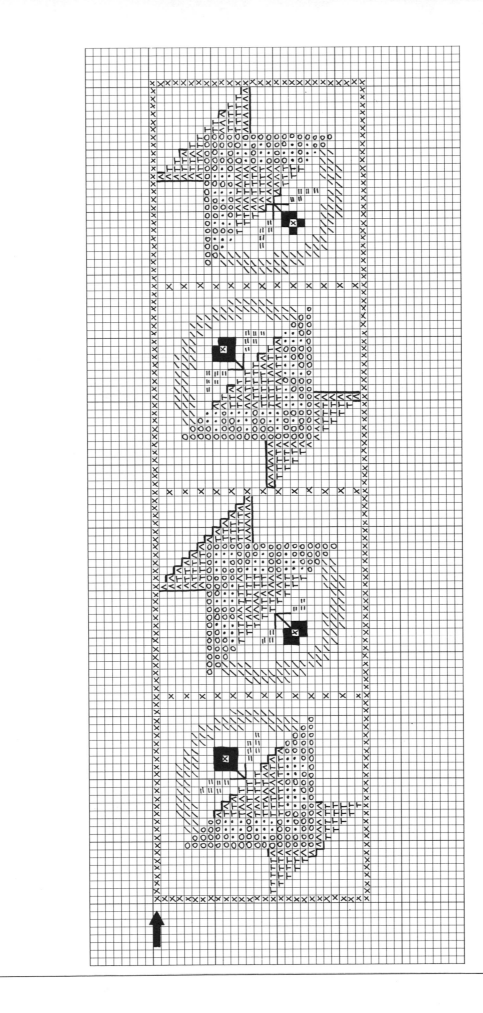

Single Bird *(In color, page C, Color Section I).*

Size: Design area approximately 4″ wide × 5½″.

Aida 14, ivory: Cut fabric 8″ wide × 9″.

Embroidery floss: Coats 2302 Orange Lt. (or DMC 743), 5000 Russet (435), 3065 Cranberry Very Dk. (600), 1001 White (Snow-White), 3127 Carnation Lt. (893), 6020 Nile Green (use Coats color), 6211 Jade Very Dk. (991), 3151 Cranberry Very Lt. (605), 3283 Rose (603), and 5472 Coffee Brown Med. (801). Purchase one skein of each.

Other materials: Flexi-Hoop pink oval frame (rubber and plastic with 4″ wide × 5½″ design area, outer dimensions 4⅝″ wide × 6⅛″ (Illus. 30), style #88582-2).

Making the first cross-stitch: Measure across 4⅛″ from top left corner; measure downwards 2″ from top left corner. Mark point where two measurements intersect. Start sewing at arrow.

Finishing directions

1. Take hoop apart. With right sides up, center inner plastic hoop over embroidery. At frequent intervals and with pencil, dot cloth 1¼″ from outside of hoop (Illus. 31). Cut cloth on dots to oval shape.
2. Stitch twice around oval, sewing ⅛″ from edges of cloth (Illus. 32).
3. With right sides up, place inner hoop flat. Center cloth on top. Add outer rubber hoop.

4. Cut piece of white floss 30″ long. While starting and ending at top of Aida, make small running stitches to gather up fabric. Sew ¼″ inside of machine-stitching (Illus. 33).
5. On back of oval, pull in on floss. Evenly adjust gathers. Tie bow; knot. Trim long ends of floss (Illus. 34).

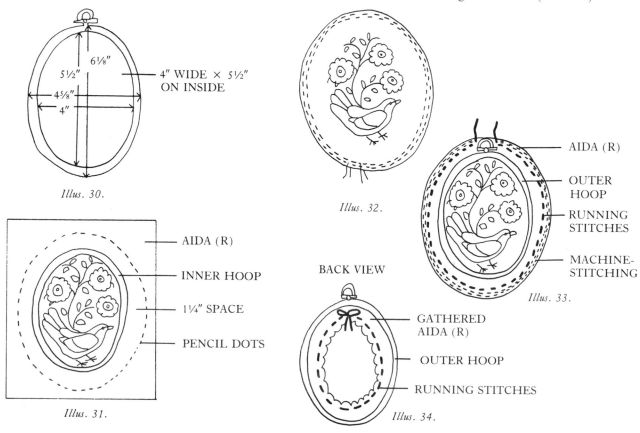

Illus. 30.

AIDA (R)
INNER HOOP
1¼″ SPACE
PENCIL DOTS

Illus. 31.

Illus. 32.

BACK VIEW

AIDA (R)
OUTER HOOP
RUNNING STITCHES
MACHINE-STITCHING

Illus. 33.

GATHERED AIDA (R)
OUTER HOOP
RUNNING STITCHES

Illus. 34.

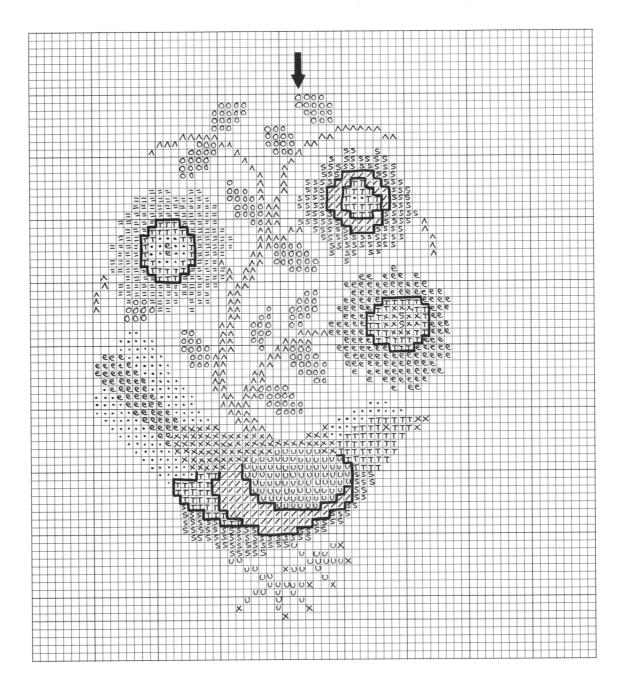

CROSS-STITCH COLOR KEY

Symbol	J. & P. Coats	DMC
T	2302 Orange Lt.	743
U	5000 Russet	435
·	3065 Cranberry Very Dk.	600
/	1001 White	Snow-White
S	3127 Carnation Lt.	893
∧	6020 Nile Green	Use J. & P. Coats color
O	6211 Jade Very Dk.	991
e	3151 Cranberry Very Lt.	605
=	3283 Rose	603
⊠	5472 Coffee Brown Med.	801
☐	Fabric as is	

BACKSTITCH COLOR KEY

Symbol	Area	J. & P. Coats	DMC
	Center of each flower and bird's wing.	5472 Coffee Brown Med.	801

Red Flowers and Yellow Birds *(In color, page G, Color Section I).*

Size: Lid approximately 8″ wide × 6″.

Irish linen, 18-thread count, unbleached: Cut fabric 11″ wide × 9″.

Embroidery floss: Coats 5360 Beige Brown Very Dk. (or DMC 898), 5365 no name (435), 2302 Orange Lt. (use Coats color), 3021 Christmas Red Dk. (498), 6267 Avocado Green (469), 5387 Cream (Ecru), 3046 Christmas Red Bright (666), and 8403 Black (310). Purchase one skein of each.

Other materials: Picture frame box by Sudberry House (hinged, woodstain with 7″ wide × 5″ design area, outer dimensions 8″ wide × 6″, style #99701). Unbleached muslin, for backing, two pieces each measuring 10½″ wide × 8½″. Eight small wire nails, ½ × 19 flat head.

Making the first cross-stitch: Measure across 2½″ from top left corner; measure downwards 2½″ from top left corner. Mark point where two measurements intersect. Start sewing at arrow.

Finishing directions

1. On embroidery, remember to stitch over two threads on linen.
2. Wash.
3. From lid, press out mounting and backing boards.
4. Center both pieces muslin over mounting board (smallest). Fold in top and bottom, then sides. Tape (Illus. 35).

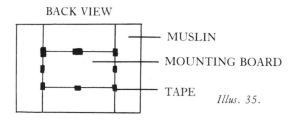

BACK VIEW

— MUSLIN

— MOUNTING BOARD

— TAPE   *Illus. 35.*

5. To embroidery, add ⅞″ margins on sides, top, and bottom. Mark with pins. Using knotted single strand of thread, hand-stitch these lines by following one row in linen and by weaving in and out cloth with 1″ running stitches (Illus. 36).

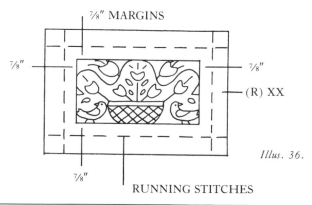

⅞″ MARGINS

⅞″

⅞″

— (R) XX

⅞″

Illus. 36.

RUNNING STITCHES

6. Repeat Steps 7–11 in "Mounting and Framing." The only exception is: At Step 7 there is no batting.
7. Place needlework inside lid. Add backing board. To permanently hold everything in position, gently hammer two nails in each side of box (Illus. 37).

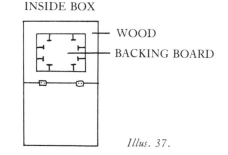

INSIDE BOX

— WOOD

— BACKING BOARD

Illus. 37.

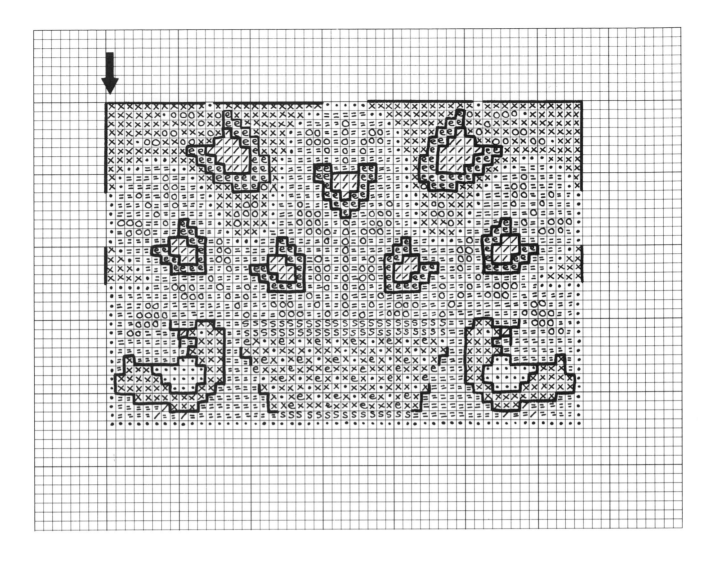

CROSS-STITCH COLOR KEY

Symbol	J. & P. Coats	DMC
·	5360 Beige Brown Very Dk.	898
S	5365 no name	435
⊠	2302 Orange Lt.	Use J. & P. Coats color
e	3021 Christmas Red Dk.	498
o	6267 Avocado Green	469
=	5387 Cream	Ecru
╱	3046 Christmas Red Bright	666
☐	Fabric as is	

BACKSTITCH COLOR KEY

Symbol	Area	J. & P. Coats	DMC
	All.	8403 Black	310

Bless This House *(In color, page K, Color Section II).*

Size: Embroidery approximately 5⅞" wide × 2⅞".

Aida 14, ivory: Premade dish towel by Charles Craft. Towel is 17⅛" wide × 27½".

Embroidery floss: Coats 7080 no name (use Coats color), 7159 Blue Very Lt. (or DMC 827), 3335 Sportsman Flesh (945), 5470 no name (433), 2326 Copper (921), 5363 Old Gold Lt. (use Coats color), 6267 Avocado Green (469), 8401 Steel Grey (318), 2300 Burnt Orange (741), and 5472 Coffee Brown Med. (898). Purchase one skein of each.

Making the first cross-stitch: See Step 1. Start sewing at arrow.

Finishing directions

1. This design is 82 stitches wide and 38 stitches high. With right sides up, fold towel in half vertically. In bottom inset, mark center crease with pin. From pin, count 41 squares of Aida to left. Mark end with pin. Towel has 40 available squares in height. Leave one blank square of Aida at top and bottom of design. Mark cloth with pins (Illus. 38 and 39). Do embroidery.
2. Wash.
3. Fold towel in thirds with embroidery centered on top.

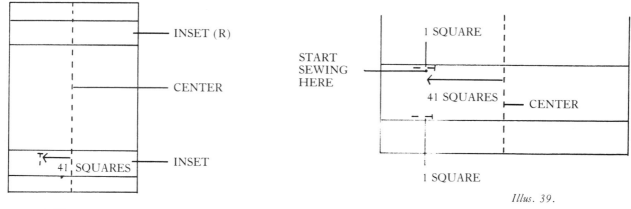

Illus. 38.

BOTTOM INSET DETAIL

Illus. 39.

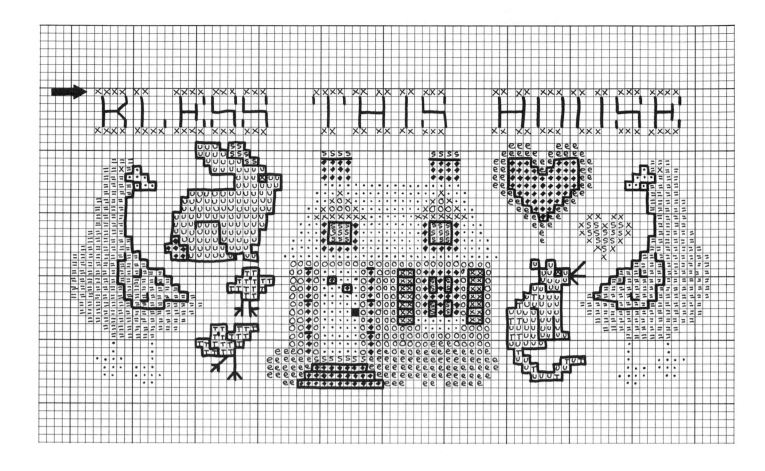

CROSS-STITCH COLOR KEY

Symbol	J. & P. Coats	DMC
⊠	7080 no name	Use J. & P. Coats color
⊡	7159 Blue Very Lt.	827
◆	3335 Sportsman Flesh	945
S	5470 no name	433
·	2326 Copper	921
≡	5363 Old Gold Lt.	Use J. & P. Coats color
e	6267 Avocado Green	469
U	8401 Steel Grey	318
T	2300 Burnt Orange	741
■	5472 Coffee Brown Med.	898
☐	Fabric as is	

BACKSTITCH COLOR KEY

Symbol	Area	J. & P. Coats	DMC
	Lettering.	7080 no name	Use J. & P. Coats color
	All other areas.	5472 Coffee Brown Med.	898

Pennsylvania Dutch *(In color, page P, Color Section II).*

Size: Embroidery on place mat approximately 2⅞" wide × 2⅝". Embroidery on napkin approximately 3¾" wide × 4¼".

Aida 14, yellow and tan: Cut yellow fabric 18" wide × 12". Cut tan fabric 14" wide × 12".

Embroidery floss: Coats 5000 Russet (or DMC 435), 5388 Beige (644), 3011 Coral (351), use DMC color (964), 7001 Peacock Blue (807), 5360 Beige Brown Very Dk. (3031), 6267 Avocado Green (469), 6266 Apple Green (3348), 4097 Violet Lt. (554), and 2307 Christmas Gold (783). Purchase one skein of each for set.

Making the first cross-stitch: See Steps 4 and 5. Start sewing at arrows.

Finishing directions

1. Fringe place mat and napkin before doing embroidery. To do this, measure ¾" from edges of both fabrics. Mark with pins. Using knotted single strands of matching thread, hand-stitch these lines by following one row in Aida and by weaving in and out cloth with ½" running stitches, pivoting at corners (Illus. 40 and 41).

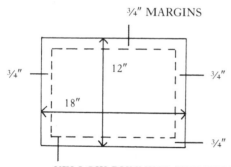

¾" MARGINS

YELLOW RUNNING STITCHES

Illus. 40.

NAPKIN (R)

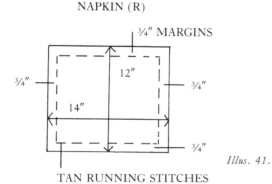

¾" MARGINS

TAN RUNNING STITCHES

Illus. 41.

2. With matching thread and sewing machine set for satin stitching (⅛" wide), stitch once around place mat and napkin. Sew over ½" running stitches. Start in middle of one side, pivoting at corners (Illus. 42).

PLACE MAT (R)

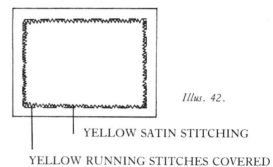

Illus. 42.

YELLOW SATIN STITCHING

YELLOW RUNNING STITCHES COVERED

3. Using big heavy needle, pull out strands of Aida one at time. Start at raw edges of fabric, and work towards satin stitching. Do sides first, then top and bottom (Illus. 43).

PLACE MAT (R)

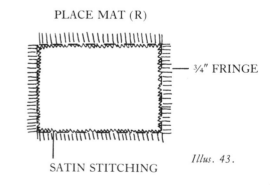

¾" FRINGE

SATIN STITCHING

Illus. 43.

4. On place mat, block off the area to be embroidered. With right sides up and working in top left corner, count in seven squares from satin stitching at top and side. Mark with pins. Using knotted single strand thread, hand-stitch these lines by following one row in Aida and by weaving in and out cloth with 1" running stitches (Illus. 44). Do embroidery here. See chart.

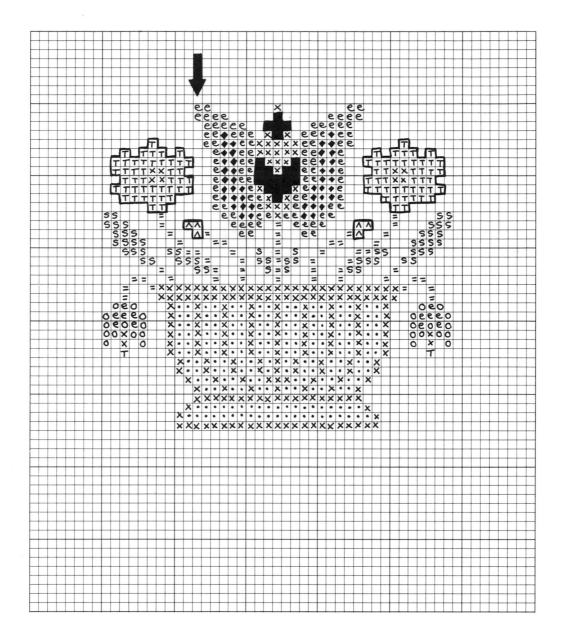

CROSS-STITCH COLOR KEY

Symbol	J. & P. Coats	DMC
·	5000 Russet	435
◆	5388 Beige	644
e	3011 Coral	351
■	Use DMC color	964
□	7001 Peacock Blue	807
⊠	5360 Beige Brown Very Dk.	3031
S	6267 Avocado Green	469
=	6266 Apple Green	3348
△	4097 Violet Lt.	554
T	2307 Christmas Gold	783
□	Fabric as is	

CROSS-STITCH COLOR KEY

Symbol	Area	J. & P. Coats	DMC
	All.	5360 Beige Brown Very Dk.	3031

Chart and instructions for napkin on page 40.

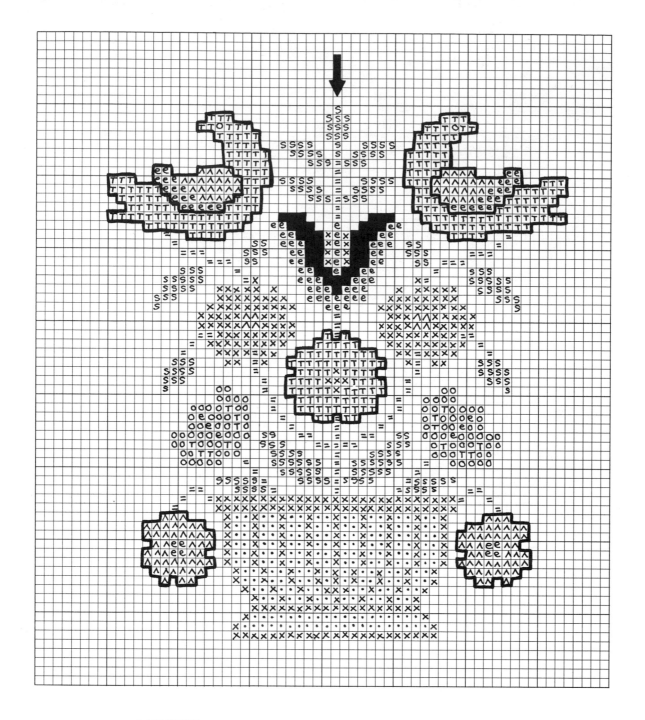

7 SQUARES

7 SQUARES

(R)

Illus. 44.

doing embroidery which corresponds to arrow in chart (Illus. 45). There are seven blank squares between finished design and satin stitching at bottom.

NAPKIN (R)

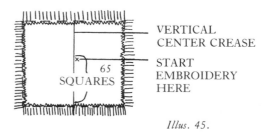

65 SQUARES

VERTICAL CENTER CREASE

START EMBROIDERY HERE

Illus. 45.

5. On napkin, locate first cross-stitch. To do so, fold napkin in half vertically. Mark center crease with pin. Open cloth. On right side of Aida and on center crease, count up 65 squares from satin stitching at bottom. At square 65, start

INTERMEDIATE PROJECTS

Spotted Dogs #1–4 *(In color, page E, Color Section I).*

Size: Four Aida insets each approximately 2¾″ in diameter.

Aida 14, white: Premade lacy jar skirts by Spinning Wheel. 2¾″ circles of Aida set in 6⅝″ circular cotton prints.

Embroidery floss: Coats 5363 Old Gold Lt. (use Coats color), 5470 no name (use Coats color), 8403 Black (or DMC 310), 7080 no name (798), 7021 Delft (809), and 3046 Christmas Red Bright (666). Purchase one skein of each for set.

Other materials: Four standard mason jars, 6-ounce size.

Making the first cross-stitch: See Steps 1 and 2. Start sewing at arrows.

Finishing directions

1. Since your Aida insets may differ in size from mine, count horizontal and vertical squares at widest part of each circle. Dog #1 is 20 stitches wide and 22 stitches high. Subtract required squares from your figures. Divide un-used squares by two. Arrange these numbers as margins (mine were seven squares on top and bottom and nine squares on sides). Mark cloth with pins. Block off the area to be embroidered. Using knotted single strand of thread, hand-stitch edges of design by following one row in Aida and by weaving in and out cloth with ½″ running stitches (Illus. 46). Refer to chart. Do embroidery.

stitches wide and 23 stitches high. Repeat same procedure in Step 1 of centering, blocking off the area to be embroidered, and embroidering.

3. Wash.

4. With right sides up, center skirts over tops of flat metal lids. Fasten metal screw bands over skirts/jars; evenly adjust gathers.

DETAIL OF AIDA INSET (R)

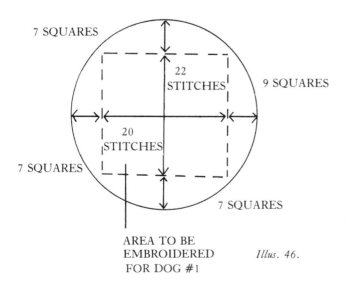

7 SQUARES

22 STITCHES

9 SQUARES

20 STITCHES

7 SQUARES

7 SQUARES

AREA TO BE EMBROIDERED FOR DOG #1

Illus. 46.

2. Dog #2 is 20 stitches wide and 24 stitches high. Dog #3 is 24 stitches wide and 22 stitches high. Dog #4 is 25

CROSS-STITCH COLOR KEY

Symbol	J. & P. Coats	DMC
⊠	5363 *Old Gold Lt.*	*Use J. & P. Coats color*
·	5470 *no name*	*Use J. & P. Coats color*
■	8403 *Black*	*310*
⚌	7080 *no name*	*798*
e	7021 *Delft*	*809*
◆	3046 *Christmas Red Bright*	*666*
☐	*Fabric as is*	

BACKSTITCH COLOR KEY

Symbol	Area	J. & P. Coats	DMC
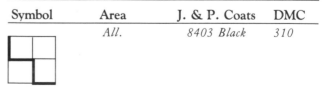	*All.*	8403 *Black*	*310*

42

basting stitches to
block out design area

basting stitches

basting stitches

basting stitches

Cow and Calf *(In color, page H, Color Section I).*

Size: Potholder approximately 8″ wide × 8½″.

Aida 14, ivory: Premade potholder by Charles Craft. Potholder is 8″ wide × 8½″.

Embroidery floss: Coats 8403 Black (or DMC 310), 5470 no name (433), 5388 Beige (644), use DMC color (611), 3006 Peach Flesh Lt. (353), and 5371 Topaz Very Ultra Dk. (437). Purchase one skein of each.

Making the first cross-stitch: See Steps 1 and 2. Start sewing at arrow.

Finishing directions

1. This design is 45 stitches high. With potholder right sides up, count down on Aida three blank squares from bias tape. Mark end with pin. Using knotted single strand of thread, hand-stitch top edge of design by following one row in Aida and by weaving in and out cloth with ½″ running stitches. From this line of running stitches, count down 45 blank squares on Aida. Mark end with pin. Stitch bottom edge of design in same manner (Illus. 47).

2. Design is 71 stitches wide and centered. In blocked off area, count horizontal squares available on your potholder. Subtract 71 from figure. Divide unused squares by two. Arrange these numbers as side margins (mine were twelve squares on left and thirteen squares on right). Mark cloth with pins. Stitch side lines as in Step 1 (Illus. 48).

3. Turn potholder upside down to make this awkward sewing easier. Refer to chart.

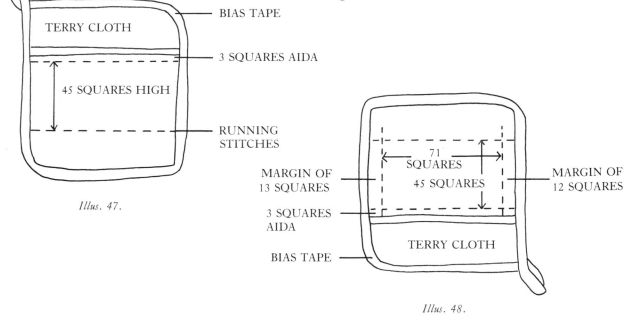

Illus. 47.

Illus. 48.

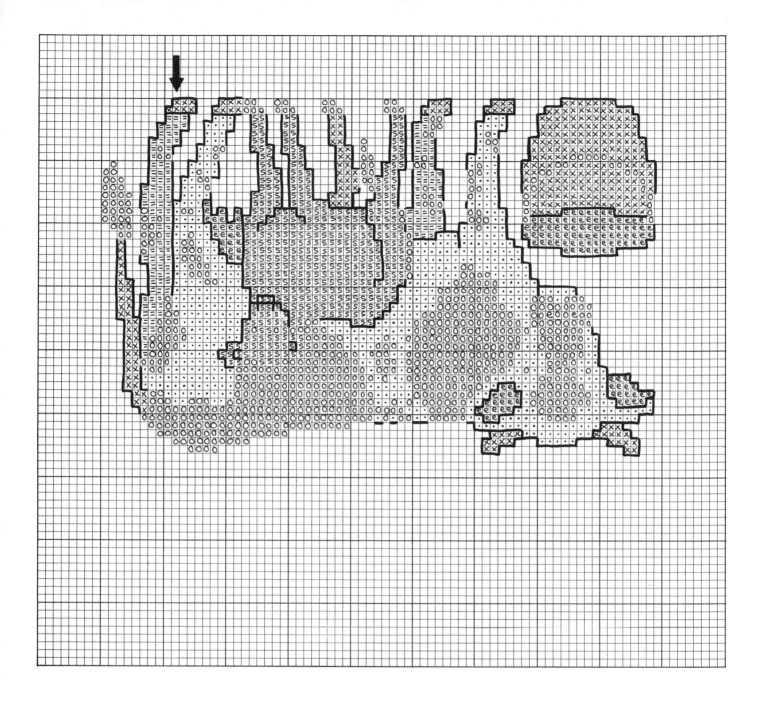

CROSS-STITCH COLOR KEY

Symbol	J. & P. Coats	DMC
⊡	8403 Black	310
⊠	5470 no name	433
·	5388 Beige	644
=	Use DMC color	611
e	3006 Peach Flesh Lt.	353
s	5371 Topaz Very Ultra Dk.	437
☐	Fabric as is	

BACKSTITCH COLOR KEY

Symbol	Area	J. & P. Coats	DMC
	All.	8403 Black	310

Potted Flowers *(In color, page A, Color Section I).*

Size: Hand towel band approximately 1⅞″ wide × 14″ without edging. Bath towel band approximately 1⅞″ wide × 24″ without edging.

Maxi-weave Ribband, 14-count, white with pink edging, 1⅞″ wide: Cut band 20″ for hand towel. Cut band 29½″ for bath towel. Purchase 1⅜ yards for set.

Embroidery floss: Coats 3153 Geranium (or DMC 956), 3065 Cranberry Very Dk. (600), 7159 Blue Very Lt. (827), 7080 no name (798), 3281 Pink Med. (3689), 4101 Violet Dk. (552), and 4104 Lavender Dk. (210). Purchase two skeins of 3153 Geranium (956). Buy one skein of each remaining color for set.

Other materials: Strawberry hand towel, 100% cotton, 16″ wide × 27½″. Strawberry bath towel, 100% cotton, 26″ wide × 49″. Flat white lace edging, ¾″ wide × 1⅜ yards for set.

Making the first cross-stitch: On hand towel, measure across 3″ (on bath towel measure across 3½″) from left end of horizontally held Ribband. Start sewing at arrows.

Finishing directions

1. For embroidery on hand towel, sew design once. Then add three more framed flowers of alternating reds and blues with single stem flowers in between. This band has total of seven framed flowers (first and last are same color) and six single-stem flowers (Illus. 49).

RIBBAND (R)

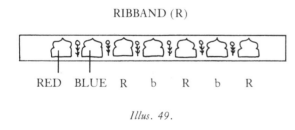

RED BLUE R b R b R

Illus. 49.

2. For embroidery on bath towel, repeat design three more times. This band has total of twelve framed flowers of alternating reds and blues (first and last are different colors) and eleven single-stem flowers (Illus. 50).

3. Cut lace into two pieces, measuring 20″ for hand and 29½″ for bath towel. With right sides up, place bottom of lace 1¾″ from bottom of each towel. At start and end, turn back ¼″ of lace; cut off excess trim. Press. Pin. Stitch lace to towel; sew ⅛″ from top edge (Illus. 51).

4. With right sides up, center each Ribband over and covering stitching in top of lace (top of Ribband is about 4″ from bottom of each towel). At start and end, turn back 1″ of Ribband. Cut off excess fabric. Press. Pin. Stitch along top, side, and bottom edges, pivoting at corners. Sew just inside pink edging (Illus. 52).

RIBBAND (R)

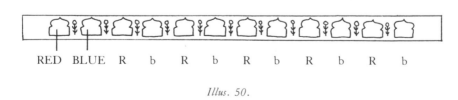

RED BLUE R b R b R b R b R b

Illus. 50.

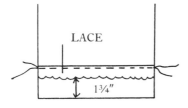

BOTTOM OF EITHER TOWEL (R)

LACE

1¾"

Illus. 51.

BOTTOM OF EITHER TOWEL (R)

RIBBAND

4"

1¾"

Illus. 52.

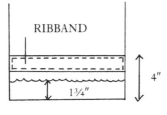

CROSS-STITCH COLOR KEY

Symbol	J. & P. Coats	DMC
⊠	3153 Geranium	956
≡	3065 Cranberry Very Dk.	600
∧	7159 Blue Very Lt.	827
e	7080 no name	798
S	3281 Pink Med.	3689
·	4101 Violet Dk.	552
■	4104 Lavender Dk.	210
☐	Fabric as is	

BACKSTITCH COLOR KEY

Symbol	Area	J. & P. Coats	DMC
	Stems on red flower.	7080 no name	798
	Stems on blue flower and lines within purple basket.	4101 Violet Dk.	552
	Lines within red basket.	3065 Cranberry Very Dk.	600

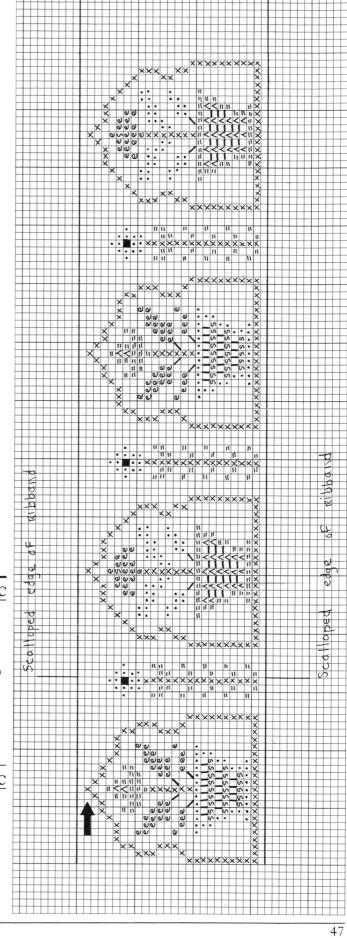

Double Ladies *(In color, page C, Color Section I).*

Size: Runner approximately 19″ wide × 13¼″.

Aida 11, white: Cut fabric 24″ wide × 18″.

Embroidery floss: Coats 7080 no name (or DMC 798), 5470 no name (433), 2302 Orange Lt. (743), 2300 Burnt Orange (741), 2307 Christmas Gold (783), 7159 Blue Very Lt. (827), 2332 Burnt Orange Dk. (608), 6266 Apple Green (3348), 6258 Willow Green (3345), and 5387 Cream (Ecru). Purchase two skeins each of 7080 no name (798) and 7159 Blue Very Lt. (827). Buy one skein of each remaining color.

Making the first cross-stitch: Measure across 2½″ from top left corner; measure downwards 2½″ from top left corner. Mark point where two measurements intersect. Start sewing at arrow A. Stitch inner blue rectangle. Then refer to arrow B.

Finishing directions

1. On four sides of Aida, count seven squares beyond outer blue rectangle. Mark with pins. Using knotted single strand white thread, hand-stitch these lines by following one row in Aida and by weaving in and out cloth with ½″ running stitches, pivoting at corners (Illus. 53).

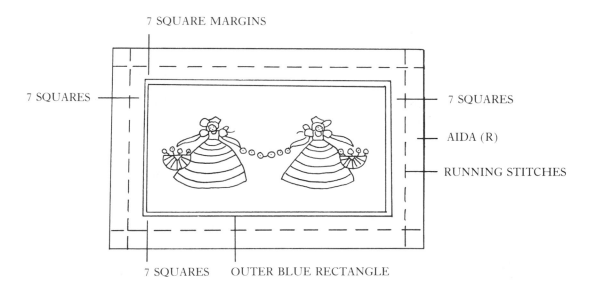

7 SQUARE MARGINS

7 SQUARES — 7 SQUARES

AIDA (R)

RUNNING STITCHES

7 SQUARES   OUTER BLUE RECTANGLE

Illus. 53.

Above: "Chickens and Eggs," page 67. Left: "Welcome," page 108.

Above: "Two
Types," page 78.
Right: "Bright Col-
ors," page 56.

Above Left: "Hearts and Tulips," page 70.
Above Right: "Bless This House," page 36.
Left: "Patterns in Repeat," page 84.

Above: "Flowers and Lace," page 114.
Right: "Cut Apple with Other Fruits," page 102.

Above: "Good
Morning, Good
Night," page 118.
Left: "Framed
Basket," page 105.

Above: "Vegetables," page 64. Right: "Teakettle and Fruit," page 122.

Above: "Hearts and Houses," page 52.
Left: "Blue Houses," page 82.

Above: "Pennsylvania Dutch," page 38.
Right: "Pastel Baskets," page 58.

2. On four sides of Aida, count another seven squares beyond running stitches. Mark with pins. Cut fabric at these points by following one row in Aida with scissor tips (Illus. 54). These seven squares will become your fringe.

3. Fringe runner. Repeat technique in Steps 2 and 3 in "Pennsylvania Dutch."

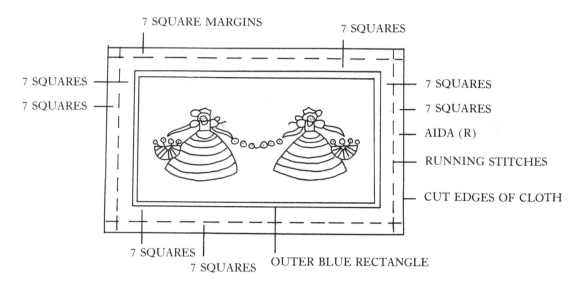

Illus. 54.

CROSS-STITCH COLOR KEY

Symbol	J. & P. Coats	DMC
⊠	7080 *no name*	798
⊟	5470 *no name*	433
⊡	2302 *Orange Lt.*	743
⊡	2300 *Burnt Orange*	741
◆	2307 *Christmas Gold*	783
·	7159 *Blue Very Lt.*	827
■	2332 *Burnt Orange Dk.*	608
⊡	6266 *Apple Green*	3348
⊡	6258 *Willow Green*	3345
⊡	5387 *Cream*	Ecru
☐	*Fabric as is*	

BACKSTITCH COLOR KEY

Symbol	Area	J. & P. Coats	DMC
	Hat rim.	7080 *no name*	798
	Lines around basket, arms, face, and 6 connecting flowers.	5470 *no name*	433

Chart on pages 50–51.

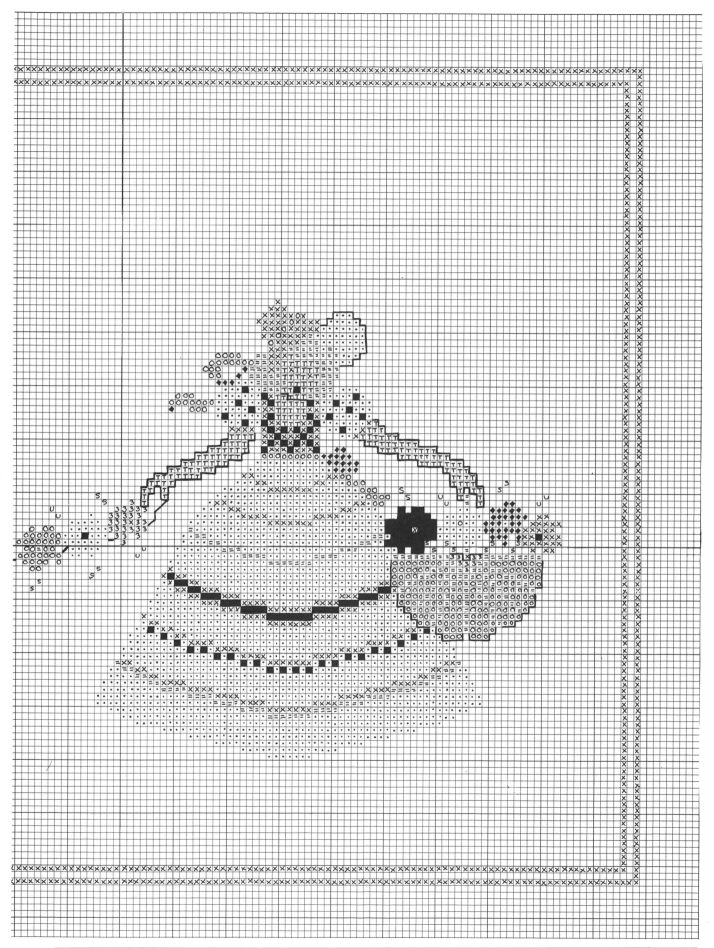

Hearts and Houses *(In color, page O, Color Section II)*.

Size: Embroidery on place mat approximately 14¾″ wide × 2¼″. Embroidery on napkin approximately 3⅝″ wide × 2¼″.

Aida 11, white: Cut place mat 20″ wide × 15″. Cut napkin 14″ square.

Embroidery floss: Coats 6256 Parrot Green Med. (or DMC 906), 2293 Yellow Dark (use Coats color), 3046 Christmas Red Bright (666), 2300 Burnt Orange (741), 3006 Peach Flesh Lt. (353), 5470 no name (801), and 6228 Christmas Green (699). Purchase two skeins of 2293 Yellow Dark (use Coats color). Purchase one skein of each remaining color for set.

Making the first cross-stitch: On place mat, measure across 2½″ from top left corner; measure downwards 2½″ from top left corner. Mark point where two measurements intersect. Start sewing at arrow. On napkin see Step 3.

Finishing directions for place mat

1. Fringe mat after embroidery is done.
2. With right sides up and on sides, count eight blank squares of Aida beyond green embroidered rectangle. On top, count five blank squares above green rectangle. On bottom measure 7¾″ below green rectangle. Mark with pins. Using knotted single strand of white thread, hand-stitch these lines by following one row in Aida and by weaving in and out cloth with ½″ running stitches, pivoting at corners (Illus. 55).

3. On four sides of mat, count another nine blank squares of Aida beyond running stitches. Mark with pins. Cut fabric at these points by following one row in Aida with scissor tips. These nine squares will become your fringe.
4. Fringe mat. Repeat technique in Steps 2 and 3 in "Pennsylvania Dutch."

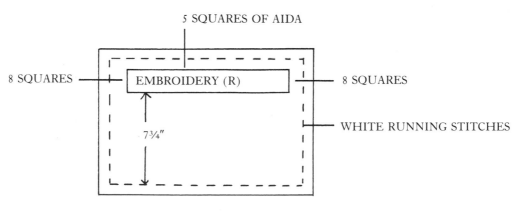

Illus. 55.

Finishing directions for napkin

1. Fringe napkin before doing embroidery. With right sides up, count nine blank squares of Aida in from all four sides of square. Mark with pins. Using knotted single strand of white thread, hand-stitch these lines by following one row in Aida and by weaving in and out of the cloth with ½" running stitches (Illus. 56).

2. Repeat technique in Steps 2 and 3 in "Pennsylvania Dutch."

3. Locate starting point for embroidery. Design is 43 stitches wide, 27 stitches high, and centered. With right sides up, fold cloth in half vertically. Mark center crease with pin. From satin stitching at bottom, count up 34 squares on Aida. Mark end with pin. On line 34, also count 21 squares to left of center crease. Mark end with pin. Start sewing here (Illus. 57). See corresponding arrow on chart. There are about seven blank squares of Aida beneath finished embroidery.

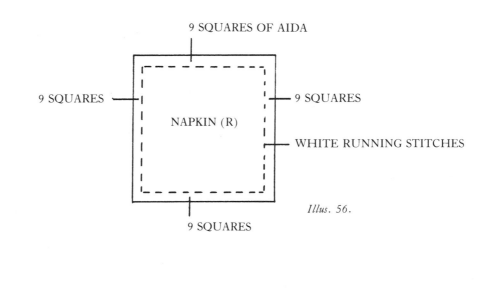

Illus. 56.

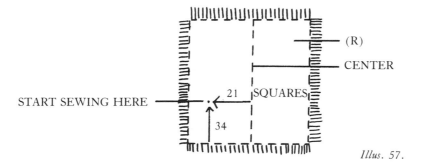

Illus. 57.

Charts and color key on pages 54–55.

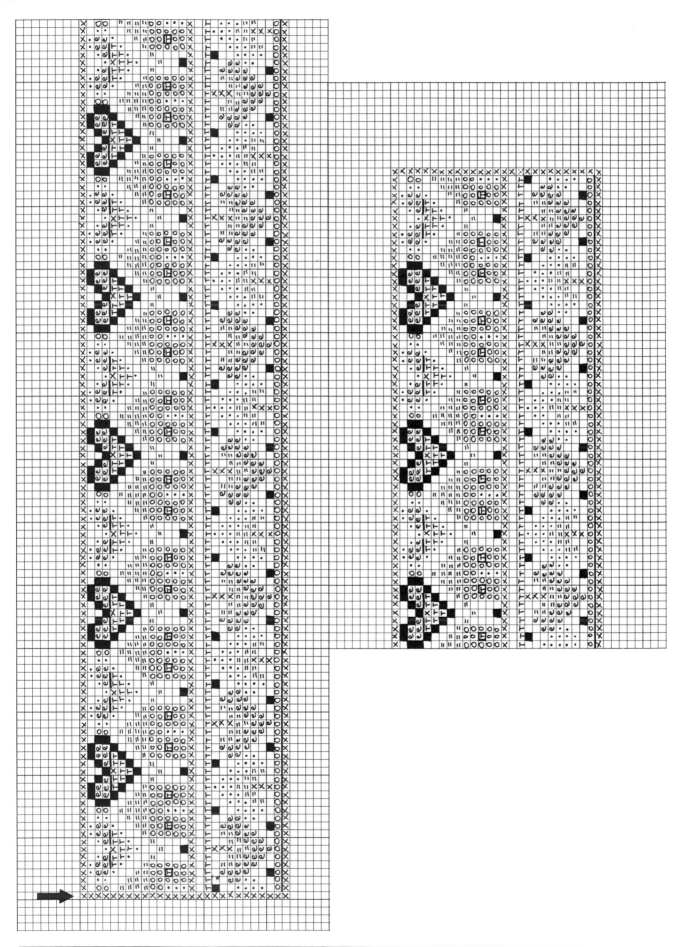

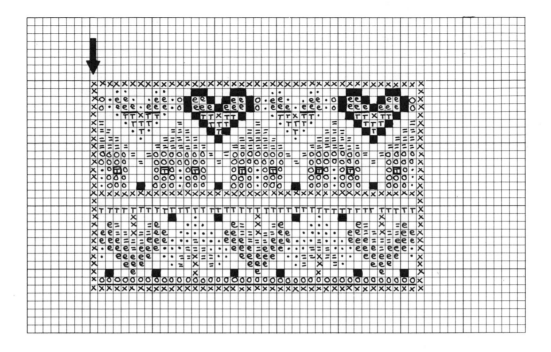

CROSS-STITCH COLOR KEY

Symbol	J. & P. Coats	DMC
⊠	6256 Parrot Green Med.	906
⊡	2293 Yellow Dark	Use J. & P. Coats color
·	3046 Christmas Red Bright	666
T	2300 Burnt Orange	741
e	3006 Peach Flesh Lt.	353
=	5470 no name	801
■	6228 Christmas Green	699
☐	Fabric as is	

BACKSTITCH COLOR KEY

Symbol	Area	J. & P. Coats	DMC
	Line in middle of top hearts.	3046 Christmas Red Bright	666
	Outline around windows.	5470 no name	801
	Line between bottom yellow and green stripe.	2300 Burnt Orange	741

Bright Colors *(In color, page J, Color Section II)*.

Size: Aida inset approximately 15″ wide × 3″.

Aida 14, white: Premade Empress hand towel by Charles Craft. Towel is 15″ wide × 26½″.

Embroidery floss: Coats 3046 Christmas Red Bright (or DMC 666), 2290 Canary Bright (307), 5471 Coffee Brown (801), 7080 no name (798), 2307 Christmas Gold (783), 7159 Blue Very Lt. (827), 6227 Christmas Green Bright (701), and 3151 Cranberry Very Lt. (957). Purchase two skeins of 3046 Christmas Red Bright (666). Buy one skein of each remaining color.

Making the first cross-stitch: See Steps 1 and 2. Start sewing at arrow.

Finishing directions

1. This design is 185 stitches wide and 38 stitches high. To center design in inset at bottom of towel, count horizontal squares available on your Aida. Subtract 185 from this number, and divide by two. Arrange this number as margins (I had eight squares) on sides of Aida (Illus. 58). Mark with pins.

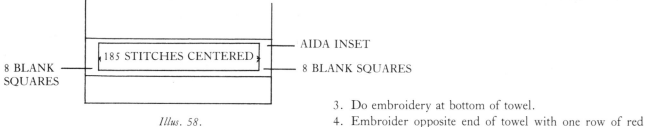

Illus. 58.

2. Center 38 stitches required for design height. In inset, count the vertical squares available on your Aida. Subtract 38 from this number and divide by two. Arrange this number as margins (I had two squares) on top and bottom of Aida (Illus. 59). Mark with pins.

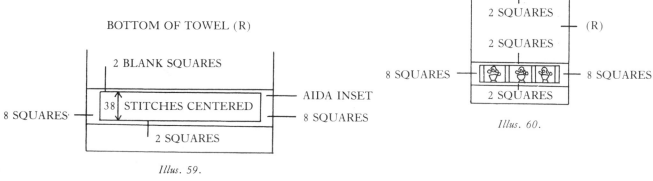

Illus. 59.

3. Do embroidery at bottom of towel.

4. Embroider opposite end of towel with one row of red cross-stitches arranged in a rectangle. Leave central area blank. Use same margins as in bottom inset (Illus. 60).

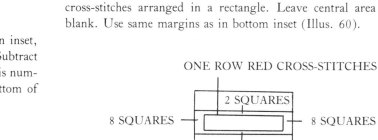

Illus. 60.

CROSS-STITCH COLOR KEY

Symbol	J. & P. Coats	DMC
⊠	3046 Christmas Red Bright	666
·	2290 Canary Bright	307
e	5471 Coffee Brown	801
S	7080 no name	798
=	2307 Christmas Gold	783
▲	7159 Blue Very Lt.	827
○	6227 Christmas Green Bright	701
△	3151 Cranberry Very Lt.	957
□	Fabric as is	

Pastel Baskets *(In color, page P, Color Section II)*.

Size: Two bands each approximately $1\frac{7}{8}''$ wide $\times$ 25″.

Maxi-weave Ribband, 14-count white with blue edging, $1\frac{7}{8}''$ wide: Cut two bands each 29″. Purchase $1\frac{7}{8}$ yards for set.

Embroidery floss: Coats 2307 Christmas Gold (or DMC 783), 2293 Yellow Dark (744), 7080 no name (798), 7159 Blue Very Lt. (827), 5471 Coffee Brown (801), 5942 Tan Brown Lt. (437), 3281 Pink Med. (963), and 3283 Rose (603). Purchase two skeins each of 2307 Christmas Gold (783) and 2293 Yellow Dark (744). Buy one skein of each remaining color for set.

Other materials: Four 1″ plastic rings.

Making the first cross-stitch: For left tieback, measure across 2″ (for right tieback measure across $12\frac{7}{8}''$) from left end of horizontally held riband (Illus. 61 and 62). Start sewing at arrows.

LEFT TIEBACK (R)

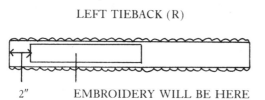

2″　　EMBROIDERY WILL BE HERE

Illus. 61.

RIGHT TIEBACK (R)

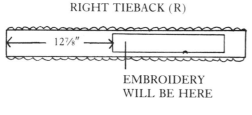

$12\frac{7}{8}''$

EMBROIDERY
WILL BE HERE

Illus. 62.

LEFT TIEBACK (R)

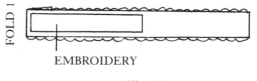

FOLD 1

EMBROIDERY

Illus. 63.

so raw edges of fabric touch fold 1. Press to create fold 2. On back of Ribband, slip-stitch top, side, and bottom edges (Illus. 64).

Finishing directions

1. Finish off left end of left tieback. With right sides up, turn Ribband back just before start of embroidery (fold 1). Press (Illus. 63). Divide Ribband that is turned back in half

LEFT TIEBACK (W)

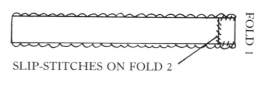

FOLD 1

SLIP-STITCHES ON FOLD 2

Illus. 64.

2. With left tieback positioned right sides up, measure 25" to right of fold 1. Pin. Turn back Ribband (fold 3). Press (Illus. 65). Divide Ribband that is turned back in half so raw edges of fabric touch fold 3. Press to create fold 4. On back of Ribband, slip-stitch top, side, and bottom edges (Illus. 66).

3. Finish off ends of right tieback. Turn tieback upside down. Repeat Steps 1 and 2.

4. Add one plastic ring to each end of tieback. To do, position rings ⅜" in from fold 1 and fold 3. Slip-stitch (Illus. 67).

LEFT TIEBACK (R)

EMBROIDERY

Illus. 65.

LEFT TIEBACK (W)

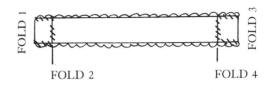

FOLD 2   FOLD 4

Illus. 66.

BACK DETAIL OF TIEBACK END

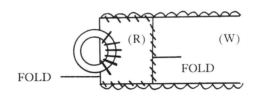

Illus. 67.

CROSS-STITCH COLOR KEY

Symbol	J. & P. Coats	DMC
⊠	2307 *Christmas Gold*	783
·	2293 *Yellow Dark*	744
e	7080 *no name*	798
≡	7159 *Blue Very Lt.*	827
□	5471 *Coffee Brown*	801
T	5942 *Tan Brown Lt.*	437
S	3281 *Pink Med.*	963
△	3283 *Rose*	603
□	*Fabric as is*	

BACKSTITCH COLOR KEY

Symbol	Area	J. & P. Coats	DMC
	Top and bottom of blue basket.	7080 *no name*	798
	Top and bottom of brown basket.	5471 *Coffee Brown*	801
	Top and bottom of pink basket.	3283 *Rose*	603

Charts on pages 60–61.

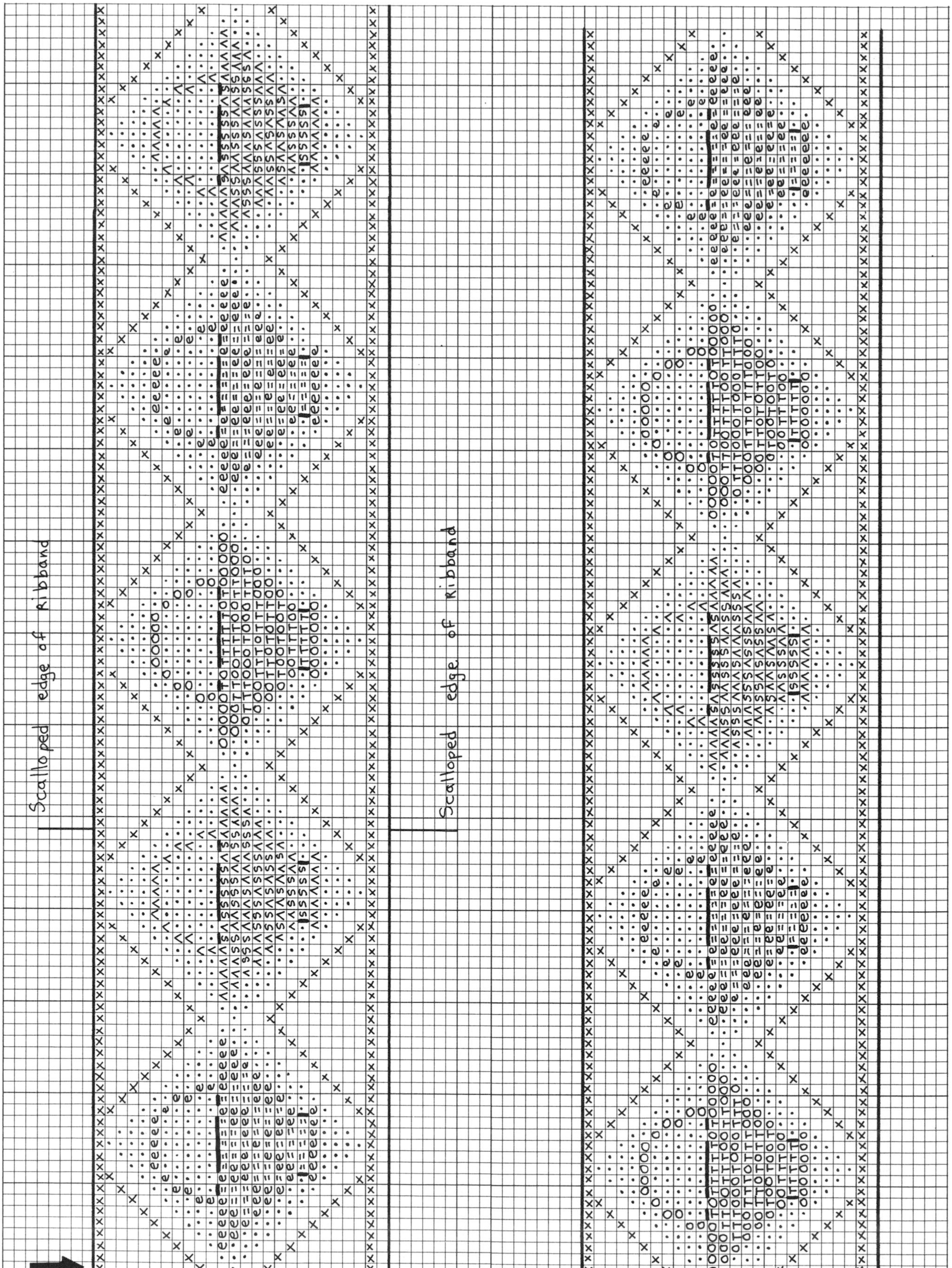
Scalloped edge of Ribband
Scalloped edge of Ribband

Scalloped edge of Ribband

Scalloped edge of Ribband

Barnyard Round-Up #1–3 *(In color, page E, Color Section 1).*

Size: Embroidery on three towels each approximately 3⅝″ wide × 2¼″.

Aida 14, two white and one blue: Premade fringed fingertip towels by Charles Craft. Each towel is 10½″ wide × 19½″.

Embroidery floss: Coats 7080 no name (or DMC 799), 5371 Topaz Very Ultra Dk. (use Coats color), 2293 Yellow Dark (744), 5471 Coffee Brown (433), 1001 White (Snow-White), 8403 Black (310), use DMC color (646), use DMC color (413), 3335 Sportsman Flesh (use Coats color), and 3283 Rose (602). Purchase one skein of each for set.

Making the first cross-stitch: See Steps 1 and 2. Start sewing at arrows.

Finishing directions

1. Each design is 29 stitches high. Before doing embroidery, make sure your inset can accommodate this. I had margins of one square at top and bottom. Mark cloth with pins.
2. Each design is 50 stitches wide. With right sides up, fold towel in half vertically. Mark crease in inset with pin. From center, count 25 squares to left. Mark end with pin. Mark point where two measurements intersect (Illus. 68). Do embroidery.
3. Wash.
4. Fold towels in thirds with embroidery centered on top.

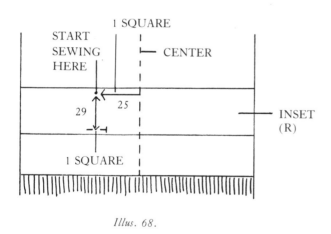

Illus. 68.

CROSS-STITCH COLOR KEY

Symbol	J. & P. Coats	DMC
⊠	7080 no name	799
⊡	5371 Topaz Very Ultra Dk.	Use J. & P. Coats color
=	2293 Yellow Dark	744
e	5471 Coffee Brown	433
U	1001 White	Snow-White
■	8403 Black	310
S	Use DMC color	646
L	Use DMC color	413
·	3335 Sportsman Flesh	Use J. & P. Coats color
T	3283 Rose	602
☐	Fabric as is	

BACKSTITCH COLOR KEY

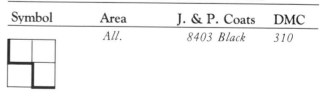

Symbol	Area	J. & P. Coats	DMC
	All.	8403 Black	310

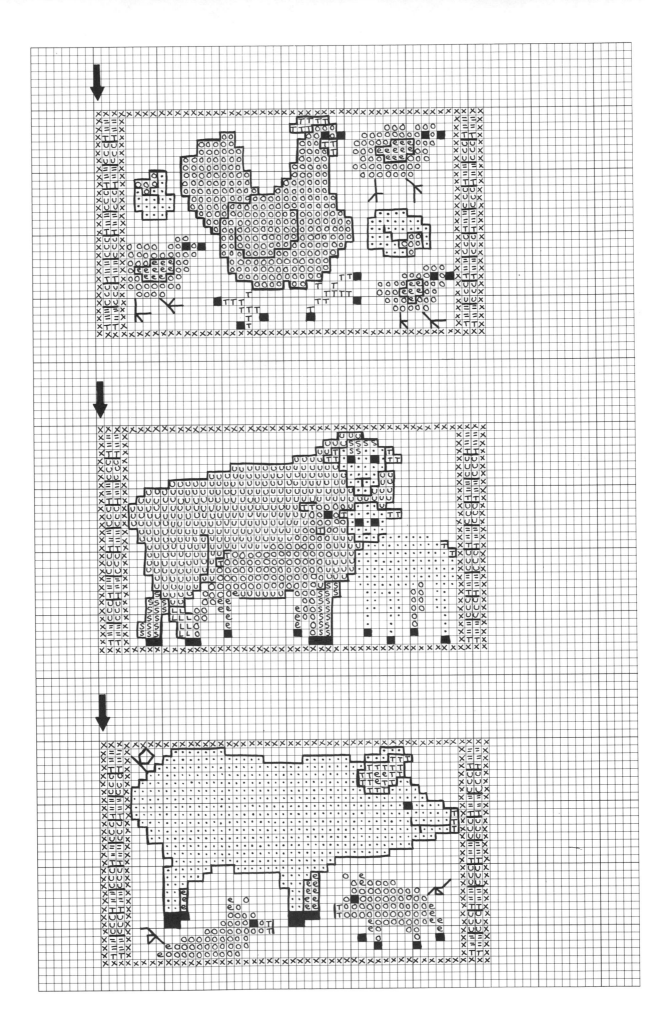

Vegetables *(In color, page N, Color Section II).*

Size: Two lids approximately 4″ and 5″ in diameter.

Perforated paper, 14-count, ivory: Cut paper 5″ square and 6″ square.

Embroidery floss: Coats 5478 Brown Very Ultra Dk. (or DMC 3371), 5000 Russet (435), 5472 Coffee Brown Med. (801), 2292 Golden Yellow Very Lt. (3078), 2290 Canary Bright (973), 2332 Burnt Orange Dk. (947), 2303 Tangerine Lt. (742), 6001 Parrot Green Lt. (907), 6227 Christmas Green Bright (701), use DMC color (3046), 2326 Copper (920), 5363 Old Gold Lt. (783), 6211 Jade Very Dk. (319), 5942 Tan Brown Lt. (437), and 6020 Nile Green (955). Purchase one skein of each for set.

Other materials: One-quart canister by Country Keepers (round walnut lid, 3⅜″ design opening, outer dimensions 4″ in diameter, style #CK 50-01). Three-quart canister by Country Keepers (round walnut lid, 4¼″ design opening, outer dimensions 5″ in diameter, style #CK 10-01). Ivory pre-gathered eyelet edging, 1⅛″ wide × 1 yard. One sheet white paper, 8½″ × 11″. White glue.

Making the first cross-stitch: On 5″ square of paper (for 4″ lid), measure across 2⅜″ from top left corner; measure downwards 1¼″ from top left corner. On 6″ square of paper (for 5″ lid), measure across 3″ from top left corner; measure downwards 1½″ from top left corner. Mark point where two measurements intersect. Start sewing at arrows.

Finishing directions

1. With right sides up, center 4″ walnut lid over 5″ square of perforated paper. With pencil, trace around edges of lid. Center 5″ lid over 6″ square of perforated paper; trace around lid. Cut out two circles.

2. On white paper, trace around two circles produced in Step 1. Cut out.

3. Assemble each lid in following manner. With right sides down, place walnut lid flat; set perforated paper inside; add circle of white paper; position plastic backing on top of pile. Glue edges of plastic backing to inside of walnut lid. Put weight on top. Let dry.

4. Glue eyelet to inside of each walnut lid. Hide eyelet heading underneath sides of lid. Overlap ends by ¾″; cut off excess trim. Let dry. Place lid on canister.

CROSS-STITCH COLOR KEY

Symbol	J. & P. Coats	DMC
◹	5478 *Brown Very Ultra Dk.*	*3371*
⊠	5000 *Russet*	*435*
L	5472 *Coffee Brown Med.*	*801*
·	2292 *Golden Yellow Very Lt.*	*3078*
⊟	2290 *Canary Bright*	*973*
■	2332 *Burnt Orange Dk.*	*947*
⋁	2303 *Tangerine Lt.*	*742*
⋀	6001 *Parrot Green Lt.*	*907*
◆	6227 *Christmas Green Bright*	*701*
S	*Use DMC color*	*3046*
◻	2326 *Copper*	*920*
⟋	5363 *Old Gold Lt.*	*783*
T	6211 *Jade Very Dk.*	*319*
U	5942 *Tan Brown Lt.*	*437*
☐	*Paper as is*	

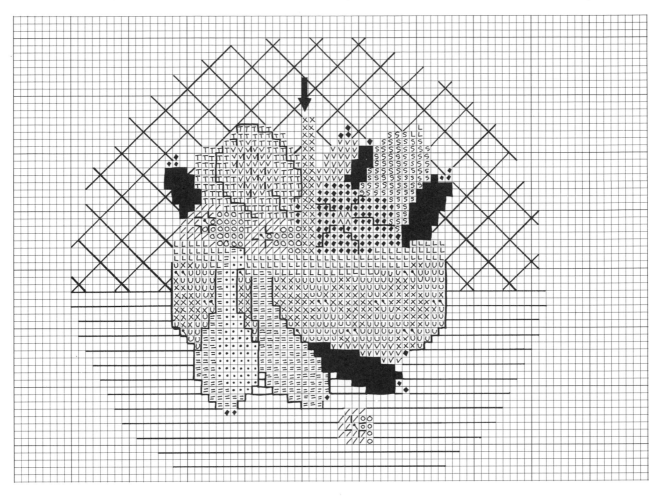

BACKSTITCH COLOR KEY

Symbol	Area	J. & P. Coats	DMC
	Large container.		
	Diamond background.	6020 Nile Green	955
	Tablecloth pattern; outline around basket; and squash outline.	5472 Coffee Brown Med.	801
	Ends of 3 onions.	5478 Brown Very Ultra Dk.	3371
	Lines within bell pepper.	2290 Canary Bright	973
	Short vertical lines within center of acorn squash.	6211 Jade Very Dk.	319
	Long lines within acorn squash.	2303 Tangerine Lt.	742
	Small container.		
	Diamond background.	6020 Nile Green	955

Area	J. & P. Coats	DMC
Tablecloth pattern.	5000 Russet	435
Outline around basket; squash outline; and lines around and within top mushroom.	5472 Coffee Brown Med.	801
Outline around 2 onions.	2326 Copper	920
Ends of 3 onions and lines around and within bottom mushroom.	5478 Brown Very Ultra Dk.	3371

Chart for small canister on following page.

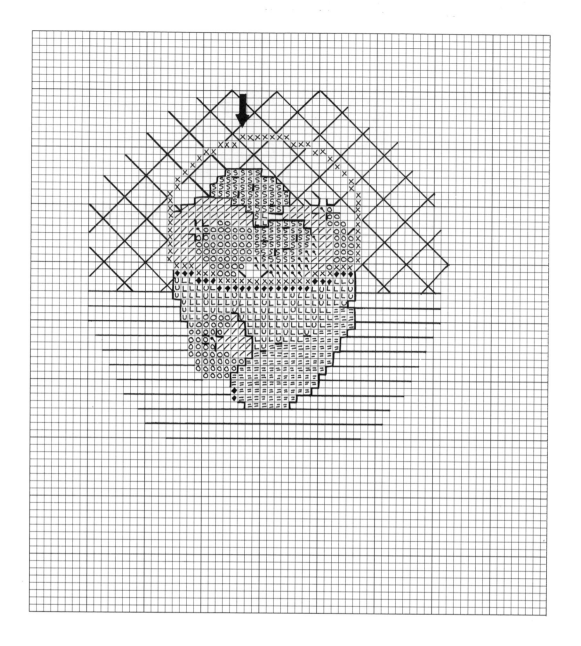

Chickens and Eggs *(In color, page 1, Color Section II)*.

Size: Skirt approximately 2¾″ wide × 40¼″.

Aida 11, white: Cut fabric 6″ wide × 44″.

Embroidery floss: Coats 2288 Lemon Lt. (or DMC 445), 3046 Christmas Red Bright (666), 8403 Black (310), 2302 Orange Lt. (743), and 1001 White (Snow-White). Purchase two skeins each of 2288 Lemon Lt. (445), 3046 Christmas Red Bright (666), and 8403 Black (310). Buy one skein of each remaining color.

Other materials: Yellow basket, 38½″ around just under top rim, 6″ high and 12½″ in diameter (Illus. 69). Red maxi piping, 1¼ yards. White elastic, ⅜″ wide × 32″.

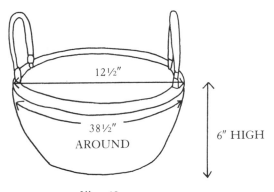

Illus. 69.

Making the first cross-stitch: Measure across 11″ from top left corner of horizontally held cloth; measure downwards 2¼″ from top left corner. Mark point where two measurements intersect. Start sewing at arrow.

Finishing directions

1. With right sides together and raw edges even, stitch ends of Aida. Make ½″ seam (Illus. 70). Press seam open.

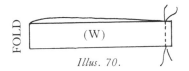

Illus. 70.

2. From bottom of black and white basket, count down three blank squares of Aida. Mark with pin. Using knotted single strand of thread, hand-stitch this line by following one row in Aida and by weaving in and out cloth with 1″ running stitches. Turn bottom of skirt towards wrong side of fabric on running stitches. Press. Trim Aida beyond fold to ⅜″ seam allowance (Illus. 71).

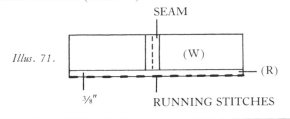

Illus. 71.

SEAM

(W)

(R)

⅜″   RUNNING STITCHES

3. Add piping to bottom of skirt. With right sides up and starting at back, place stitching on piping under the folded edge of Aida. Turn ends of piping upwards at start and finish; overlap ends by 1½″. Pin. Hand-baste. Stitch close to folded edge of Aida (Illus. 72).

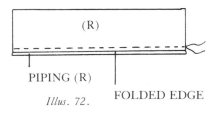

(R)

PIPING (R)

Illus. 72.   FOLDED EDGE

4. With right sides up, prepare top of skirt for completion. First, at top of chicken with red crown, count up seven blank squares of Aida. Mark with pin. Using knotted single strand of white thread, hand-stitch this line by following one row in Aida and by weaving in and out cloth with 1″ running stitches. Call this line fold 1. Second, above fold 1 count up an additional six blank squares of Aida. Mark with pin. Hand-stitch this line in the same manner; call this fold 2. Trim fabric above fold 2 to ¼″ seam allowance (Illus. 73).

5. At top of skirt, make casing for elastic. On fold 2, turn ¼″ seam allowance back towards the wrong side of the fabric. Press. Turn Aida back again towards wrong side of fabric on fold 1. Press. Pin. Stitch close to fold 2, leaving 2″ opening in middle of back (Illus. 74).

SKIRT DETAIL (R)

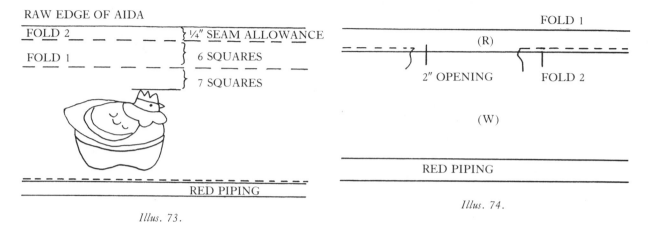

RAW EDGE OF AIDA

FOLD 2 _ _ _ _ _ _ ¼" SEAM ALLOWANCE

FOLD 1 _ _ _ _ _ 6 SQUARES

7 SQUARES

RED PIPING

Illus. 73.

SKIRT DETAIL (W)

FOLD 1

(R)

2" OPENING   FOLD 2

(W)

RED PIPING

Illus. 74.

6. Attach safety pin to one end of the elastic. Insert elastic through opening in casing, and slide safety pin through. Overlap ends of elastic by 1". Stitch.

7. Stitch opening in casing closed.

8. Center skirt on basket under rim.

CROSS-STITCH COLOR KEY

Symbol	J. & P. Coats	DMC
⋅	2288 Lemon Lt.	445
⊠	3046 Christmas Red Bright	666
≡	8403 Black	310
◆	2302 Orange Lt.	743
⊙	1001 White	Snow-White
☐	Fabric as is	

BACKSTITCH COLOR KEY

Symbol	Area	J. & P. Coats	DMC
	All.	8403 Black	310

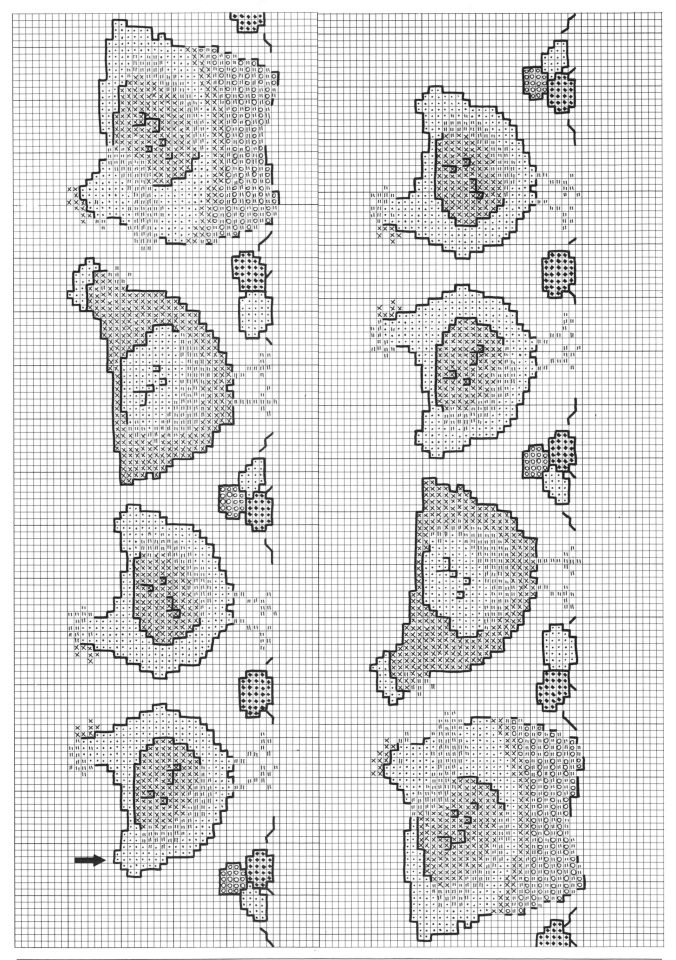

Hearts and Tulips *(In color, page K, Color Section II).*

Size: Hanging approximately 5″ wide × 14¾″.

Aida 11, ivory: Cut fabric 8″ wide × 19″.

Embroidery floss: Coats 2307 Christmas Gold (or DMC 783), use DMC color (761), 3283 Rose (603), 3021 Christmas Red Dk. (498), use DMC color (917), use DMC color (793), use DMC color (581), use DMC color (991), 5470 no name (433), 5472 Coffee Brown Med. (898), use DMC color (611), and 5387 Cream (Ecru). Purchase one skein of each.

Other materials: Unbleached muslin, for back, 6¼″ wide × 17½″. Brass hardware, 5⁹⁄₁₆″ wide (cloth fits into 5³⁄₁₆″ space on back) × ⁹⁄₁₆″ (not including decorative circles).

Making the first cross-stitch: Measure across 3⅝″ from top left corner; measure downwards 3¼″ from top left corner. Mark point where two measurements intersect. Start sewing at arrow.

Finishing directions
1. Make bell pull pattern (Illus. 75).
2. With right sides up, place pattern over embroidery. Center design so that sides and top and bottom are equal (Illus. 76). Pin. Cut. Transfer stitching lines to the wrong side of front.

BELL PULL

FRONT: CUT ONE, EMBROIDERED AIDA

BACK: CUT ONE, MUSLIN

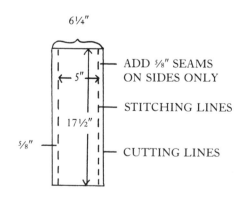

6¼″

ADD ⅝″ SEAMS ON SIDES ONLY

5″

STITCHING LINES

17½″

CUTTING LINES

⅝″

Illus. 75.

3. Lay out and cut back. Before pattern is unpinned, transfer stitching lines to wrong side.

TRACING PAPER PATTERN PINNED ON TOP WITH DESIGN CENTERED UNDERNEATH

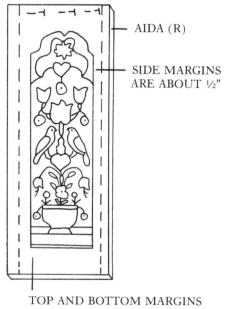

AIDA (R)

SIDE MARGINS ARE ABOUT ½″

TOP AND BOTTOM MARGINS ARE ABOUT 2⅜″

Illus. 76.

4. With right sides together and seams matching, pin front to back. Stitch sides (Illus. 77). Trim seams to ⅜". Turn. Press.

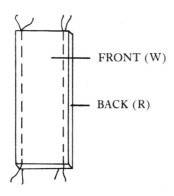

Illus. 77.

5. Finish off ends of bell pull. To prevent unravelling, stitch twice across top and bottom edges. Then, at top, measure 1¼" above embroidered arch, and at bottom, measure 1¼" beneath embroidery. Mark with pins. Press front towards back along both these points (Illus. 78).

MACHINE-STITCHING

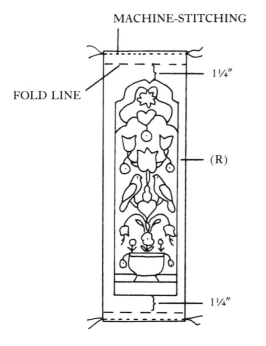

FOLD LINE

1¼"

(R)

1¼"

Illus. 78.

6. Slip-stitch ends of bell pull to back (Illus. 79).

FOLDED TOP EDGE

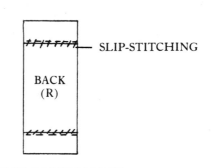

SLIP-STITCHING

BACK (R)

Illus. 79.

FOLDED BOTTOM EDGE

7. Add hardware. At top, push folded end of fabric through space in back of brass. Insert cross bar through sleeve, and pull down on cloth. Repeat at bottom (Illus. 80).

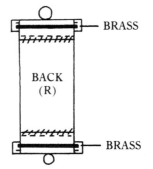

BRASS

BACK (R)

BRASS

Illus. 80.

Chart and color key on pages 72–73.

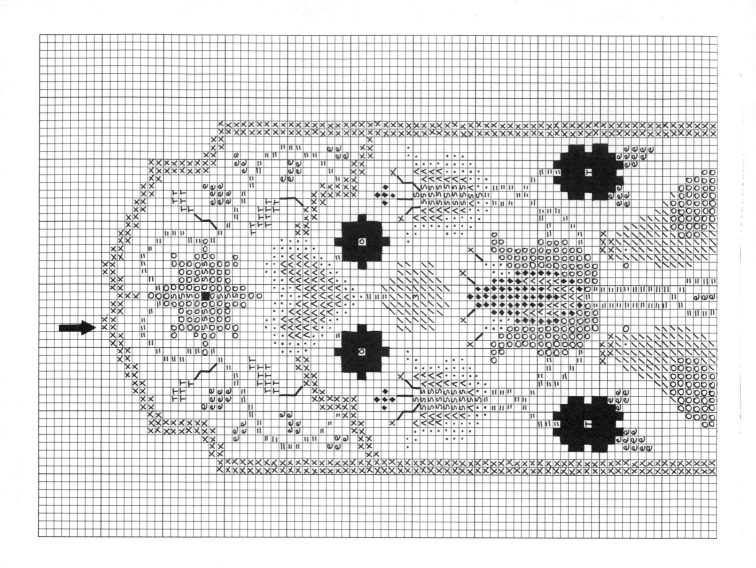

CROSS-STITCH COLOR KEY

Symbol	J. & P. Coats	DMC
○	2307 Christmas Gold	783
△	Use DMC color	761
T	3283 Rose	603
·	3021 Christmas Red Dk.	498
S	Use DMC color	917
╱	Use DMC color	793
=	Use DMC color	581
e	Use DMC color	991
⊠	5470 no name	433
■	5472 Coffee Brown Med.	898
◆	Use DMC color	611
3	5387 Cream	Ecru
□	Fabric as is	

BACKSTITCH COLOR KEY

Symbol	Area	J. & P. Coats	DMC
	Bud stems, leaf stems, and flower pistons.	Use DMC color	991
	Bird legs.	5472 Coffee Brown Med.	898
	Lines around and within the basket.	3021 Christmas Red Dk.	498

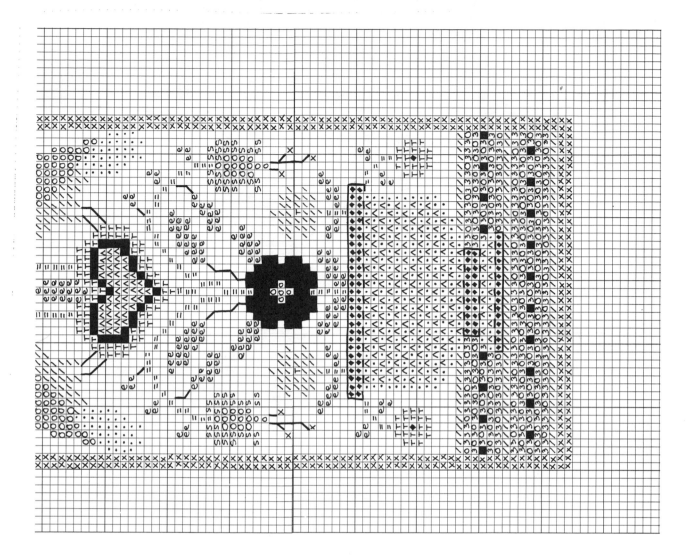

ADVANCED PROJECTS

Painted Basket *(In color, page B, Color Section 1).*

Size: Frame approximately 6″ square.

Perforated paper, 14-count, ivory: Cut paper 6″ square.

Embroidery floss: Coats 5471 Coffee Brown (or DMC 801), 4092 Violet Med. (552), 4104 Lavender Dk. (210), 2290 Canary Bright (307), 2300 Burnt Orange (741), 3001 Cranberry Lt. (605), use DMC color (915), 7001 Peacock Blue (807), 1001 White (Snow-White), 3281 Pink Med. (818), 3056 Watermelon (use Coats color), 7080 no name (798), 5365 no name (436), 5478 Brown Very Ultra Dk. (3371), 5388 Beige (644), 6020 Nile Green (955), and 6258 Willow Green (3345). Purchase one skein of each.

Other materials: Frame (woodstain with design area of 4¾″ square, outer dimensions of 6″ square, and back opening of 5⅛″ square) Illus. 81 and 82. White mat board, 7″ square. Sawtooth picture hanger. Eight small wire nails, ½ × 19 flat head.

tern at sides and bottom of design are very narrow, approximately ⅛″. Check dimensions of your frame before paper is cut.

2. Cut mat board same size as perforated paper.

3. Assemble picture in frame. With right sides down, place frame flat, add perforated paper, and mat board. To permanently hold everything in position, gently hammer two nails in each side of frame. On back of frame, center sawtooth picture hanger along top edge.

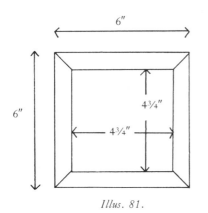

Illus. 81.

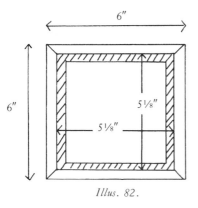

Illus. 82.

Making the first cross-stitch: Measure across 2⅛″ from top left corner; measure downwards ¾″ from top left corner. Mark point where two measurements intersect. Start sewing at arrow.

Finishing directions

1. Cut perforated paper down to 5⅛″ square (precise size of opening in back of frame). Margins beyond diamond pat-

CROSS-STITCH COLOR KEY

Symbol	J. & P. Coats	DMC
C	5471 Coffee Brown	801
=	4092 Violet Med.	552
o	4104 Lavender Dk.	210
■	2290 Canary Bright	307
◆	2300 Burnt Orange	741
⊠	3001 Cranberry Lt.	605
T	Use DMC color	915
e	7001 Peacock Blue	807
U	1001 White	Snow-White
/	3281 Pink Med.	818
△	3056 Watermelon	Use J. & P. Coats color
◤	7080 no name	798
S	5365 no name	436
Z	5478 Brown Very Ultra Dk.	3371
L	5388 Beige	644
·	6020 Nile Green	955
3	6258 Willow Green	3345
☐	Paper as is	

BACKSTITCH COLOR KEY

Symbol	Area	J. & P. Coats	DMC
	Outline around light pink flower on left and tips of dark pink flower on right.	*3056 Watermelon*	*Use J. & P. Coats color*
	Outline around light pink flower on right.	*Use DMC color*	*915*
	All basket details.	*5478 Brown Very Ultra Dk.*	*3371*

Two Types *(In color, page J, Color Section II).*

Size: Four squares of embroidery each approximately 2½″ wide × 3″.

Hopscotch, 14-count Aida, brown and oatmeal combination: Cut fabric by Charles Craft 15″ square.

Embroidery floss: Coats 7976 Baby Blue (or DMC 800), 2300 Burnt Orange (741), 7080 no name (798), 3046 Christmas Red Bright (666), 3021 Christmas Red Dk. (816), 2288 Lemon Lt. (307), 3281 Pink Med. (818), 3153 Geranium (956), 7001 Peacock Blue (use Coats color), 4104 Lavender Dk. (210), 3011 Coral (351), 5371 Topaz Very Ultra Dk. (436), 5387 Cream (Ecru), 6256 Parrot Green Med. (906), 6020 Nile Green (955), 8403 Black (310), and 5472 Coffee Brown Med. (801). Purchase one skein of each.

Other materials: Brown maxi piping, 1¾ yards.

Making the first cross-stitch: See Steps 4 and 5. Start sewing at arrows.

Finishing directions

1. Finish off raw edges of Aida before doing embroidery. To do, with right sides down, turn cloth back ¼″ on all sides. Fold in top and bottom, then sides. Press.
2. Baste piping to Hopscotch. Begin 3½″ from one corner. Position folded edge of piping away from design. Turn end upwards at start, and arrange so stitching on piping is covered by folded edges of Hopscotch, pivoting at corners. Overlap ends by ¾″; turn end upwards (Illus. 83).
3. With right sides up, stitch piping to Hopscotch. Stitch closely to the folded edge of cloth, pivoting at corners. Stitch again ⅛″ to inside of first stitching (Illus. 84).
4. Fold cloth, as shown. Embroidery is positioned within four solid brown areas, and each design is 37 stitches wide and 42 stitches high. To make embroidery easier, block off

these areas by referring to diagram. Count off designated blank squares of Aida. Mark with pins. On sides that are starred, make sure these margins do not vary. Then using knotted single strand of thread, hand-stitch these points by following one row in Aida and by weaving in and out cloth with ½″ running stitches (Illus. 85).
5. In top half of cloth, embroider baskets 1 and 2. Turn cloth upside down, and repeat baskets again (Illus. 86).

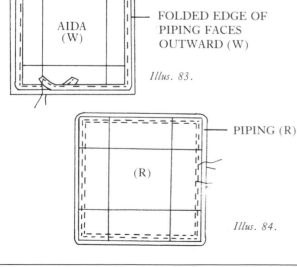

Illus. 83.

Illus. 84.

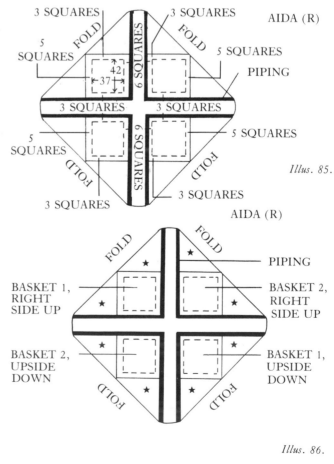

Illus. 85.

Illus. 86.

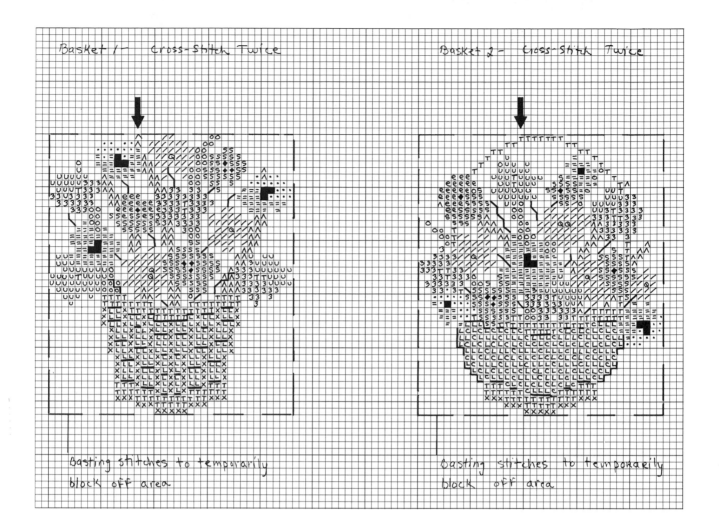

CROSS-STITCH COLOR KEY

Symbol	J. & P. Coats	DMC
·	7976 Baby Blue	800
■	2300 Burnt Orange	741
=	7080 no name	798
U	3046 Christmas Red Bright	666
3	3021 Christmas Red Dk.	816
T	2288 Lemon Lt.	307
e	3281 Pink Med.	818
S	3153 Geranium	956
◆	7001 Peacock Blue	Use J. & P. Coats color
/	4104 Lavender Dk.	210
Q	3011 Coral	351
⊠	5371 Topaz Very Ultra Dk.	436
L	5387 Cream	Ecru
∧	6256 Parrot Green Med.	906
○	6020 Nile Green	955
C	8403 Black	310
□	Fabric as is	

BACKSTITCH COLOR KEY

Symbol	Area	J. & P. Coats	DMC
	All flower stems and outline around black basket.	8403 Black	310
	Lines within tan basket.	5472 Coffee Brown Med.	801

Strawberries

Size: Wreath approximately 8½″ in diameter.

Fiddler's Cloth, 14-count, oatmeal: Cut fabric by Charles Craft 11″ square.

Embroidery floss: Coats 5360 Beige Brown Very Dk. (or DMC 898), 5371 Topaz Very Ultra Dk. (use Coats color), 5470 no name (use Coats color), 2293 Yellow Dark (744), 3046 Christmas Red Bright (666), 3021 Christmas Red Dk. (498), 6227 Christmas Green Bright (701), and 6238 Chartreuse Bright (704). Purchase one skein of each.

Other materials: Grapevine wreath (8½″ in diameter on outside with design area of 6″ in diameter). Muslin, for backing, 11″ square. Stitch Witchery, 11″ square. Grey cardboard, for backing, 10″ square. Red satin ribbon, double-faced, ⅛″ wide × 3½ yards. Tracing paper, 9″ wide × 12″. One round head brass paper fastener, ½″ long. Compass. White glue.

Making the first cross-stitch: Measure across 5¼″ from top left corner; measure downwards 3″ from top left corner. Mark point where two measurements intersect. Start sewing at arrow.

Finishing directions

1. Bond Fiddler's Cloth to muslin with Stitch Witchery. With right sides up, place muslin flat, add Stitch Witchery, and position embroidery on top. Line up edges. Follow Stitch Witchery directions for bonding. Test for adhesion. Let fabric cool.
2. With right sides up, place wreath over tracing paper. Trace around outer edges. With compass, draw second circle ⅜″ to inside. Then divide circle into four equal quarters by folding and creasing (Illus. 87). Cut out inner circle.

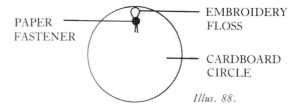

PAPER FASTENER — EMBROIDERY FLOSS — CARDBOARD CIRCLE

Illus. 88.

TRACING PAPER (R)

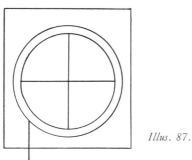

Illus. 87.

OUTER EDGE OF WREATH

3. With right sides up, place paper circle over Fiddler's combination. Use quarter segments in circle as guidelines to center paper over embroidery. Pin. Cut Fiddler's combination and cardboard to size of paper.
4. Push paper fastener through top of cardboard circle, 1″ from outer edge. Open brass legs, and spread flat. Take 4″ piece of floss, and knot twice 1″ from ends. To hang wreath, attach loop to brass fastener (Illus. 88).

5. Glue Fiddler's combination to cardboard. Spread glue ½″ from outer edges of cardboard. Put weight on top. Let dry.
6. Cut ribbon into two pieces, measuring 1½ and 2 yards.
7. With 2-yard length, wrap ribbon around wreath. Double-knot the ends at top front. Single-knot the ends of ribbon, and let hang (Illus. 89).

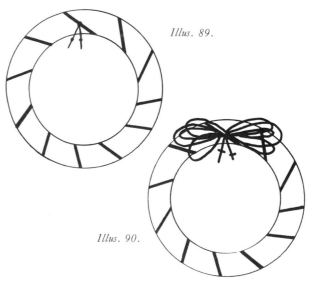

Illus. 89.

Illus. 90.

8. With 1½-yard length, make bow. Loop ribbon back and forth between 5″ width. Center bow over top of wreath; double-knot. Single-knot the ends of ribbon, and let hang (Illus. 90).

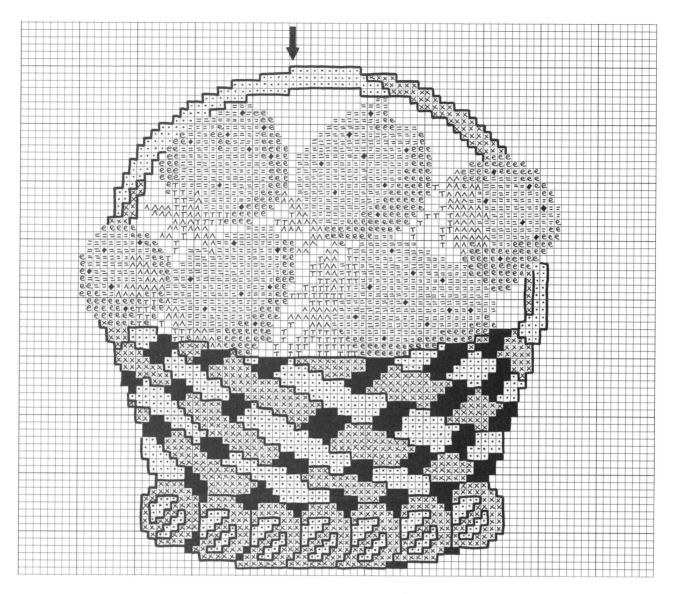

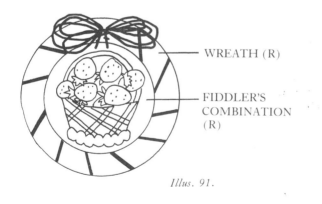

Illus. 91.

9. With right sides up, center wreath over Fiddler's combination. Spread glue ½″ from outer edges of both wreath and Fiddler's combination. Put weight on top. Let dry (Illus. 91).

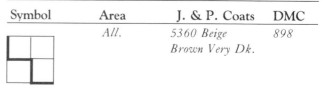

CROSS-STITCH COLOR KEY

Symbol	J. & P. Coats	DMC
■	5360 Beige Brown Very Dk.	898
⊠	5371 Topaz Very Ultra Dk.	Use J. & P. Coats color
·	5470 no name	Use J. & P. Coats color
◆	2293 Yellow Dark	744
=	3046 Christmas Red Bright	666
e	3021 Christmas Red Dk.	498
T	6227 Christmas Green Bright	701
∧	6238 Chartreuse Bright	704
☐	Fabric as is	

BACKSTITCH COLOR KEY

Symbol	Area	J. & P. Coats	DMC
	All.	5360 Beige Brown Very Dk.	898

Blue Houses *(In color, page O, Color Section II).*

Size: Embroidery approximately 14¾″ wide × 14½″.

Aida 8, ivory: Cut fabric 32″ square.

Embroidery floss: Coats 7981 Navy Blue (use Coats color), 5000 Russet (or DMC 435), 7080 no name (799), 7976 Baby Blue (775), 7100 Royal Blue Dk. (796), 7021 Delft (809), and 7023 Blue Med. (use Coats color). Purchase six skeins of 7981 Navy Blue (use Coats color) and three skeins of 7080 no name (799). Shop for two skeins of 5000 Russet (435). Buy one skein of each remaining color.

Making the first cross-stitch: Measure across 8½″ from top left corner; measure downwards 8½″ from top left corner. Mark point where two measurements intersect. Start sewing at arrow.

Finishing directions

1. Prepare cloth for fringing. From four sides of navy border, measure 6½″ outwards. Mark with pins. Check that all 6½″ margins have same number of blank squares of Aida. Connect these four points. Using knotted single strand of ivory thread, hand-stitch these lines by following one row in Aida and by weaving in and out cloth with ½″ running stitches (Illus. 92).
2. Fringe cloth. Repeat technique in Step 2 in "Pennsylvania Dutch." The only exception is: This satin stitch is 3/16″ wide.
3. Measure 1″ beyond satin stitching. Mark cloth with pins. Cut off excess fabric by following one row in Aida.
4. Repeat Step 3 in "Pennsylvania Dutch."

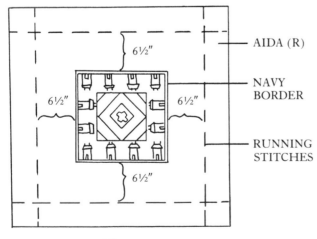

Illus. 92.

CROSS-STITCH COLOR KEY

Symbol	J. & P. Coats	DMC
⊠	7981 Navy Blue	Use J. & P. Coats color
·	5000 Russet	435
▢	7080 no name	799
▤	7976 Baby Blue	775
△	7100 Royal Blue Dk.	796
▣	7021 Delft	809
◆	7023 Blue Med.	Use J. & P. Coats color
▢	Fabric as is	

BACKSTITCH COLOR KEY

Symbol	Area	J. & P. Coats	DMC
	All.	7981 Navy Blue	Use J. & P. Coats color

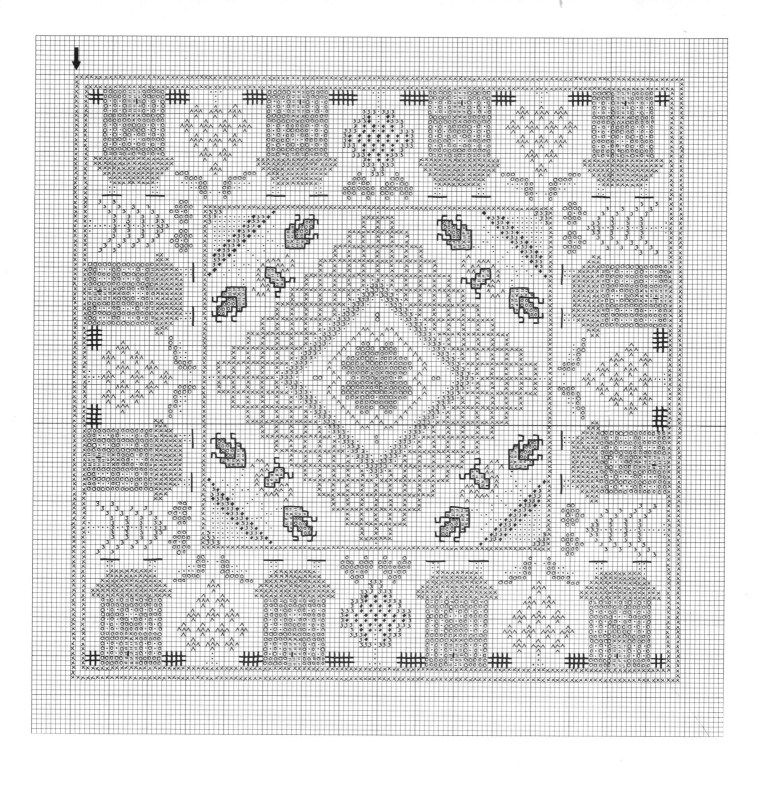

Patterns in Repeat *(In color, page K, Color Section II).*

Size: Tray approximateely 12″ wide × 9″.

Aida 14, ivory: Cut fabric 15″ wide × 12″.

Embroidery floss: Coats 5000 Russet (or DMC 435), 6267 Avocado Green (469), 2326 Copper (920), 5363 Old Gold Lt. (use Coats color), 5360 Beige Brown Very Dk. (838), and 5387 Cream (Ecru). Purchase two skeins each of 5000 Russet (435), 6267 Avocado Green (469), 2326 Copper (920), and 5360 Beige Brown Very Dk. (838). Buy one skein of each remaining color.

Other materials: Petite tray by Sudberry House (wood-stain with 10″ wide × 7″ rectangle mat, outer dimensions 12″ wide × 9″, classic style #65651). Unbleached muslin, for backing, 15″ wide × 12″. Stitch Witchery, 15″ wide × 12″.

Making the first cross-stitch: Measure across 3″ from top left corner; measure downwards 3″ from top left corner. Mark point where two measurements intersect. Start sewing at arrow.

Finishing directions

1. Repeat Step 1 in "Strawberries." The only exception is: You are working with Aida.
2. Remove screws at one end of tray. Slide-out wooden mat, cardboard, and base. Glass is inside. Handle with care; clean.
3. With right sides up, center rectangle mat over Aida/ Stitch Witchery/muslin combination. Get margins equal at sides (mine are about ¹¹⁄₁₆″) and at top and bottom (mine are about ⁹⁄₁₆″). With pencil trace around outer edge of mat. Cut fabric.
4. With right sides up, tape Aida combination to cardboard in north-south-east-west position.
5. Reassemble frame. Working from bottom to top, slide-in base (wrong side up), Aida/cardboard combination (right side up), wooden mat (right side up), and glass on top.
6. Replace end of tray.

CROSS-STITCH COLOR KEY

Symbol	J. & P. Coats	DMC
⊡	5000 Russet	435
·	6267 Avocado Green	469
⊟	2326 Copper	920
T	5363 Old Gold Lt.	Use J. & P. Coats color
⊠	5360 Beige Brown Very Dk.	838
◆	5387 Cream	Ecru
☐	Fabric as is	

BACKSTITCH COLOR KEY

Symbol	Area	J. & P. Coats	DMC
	All.	5360 Beige Brown Very Dk.	838

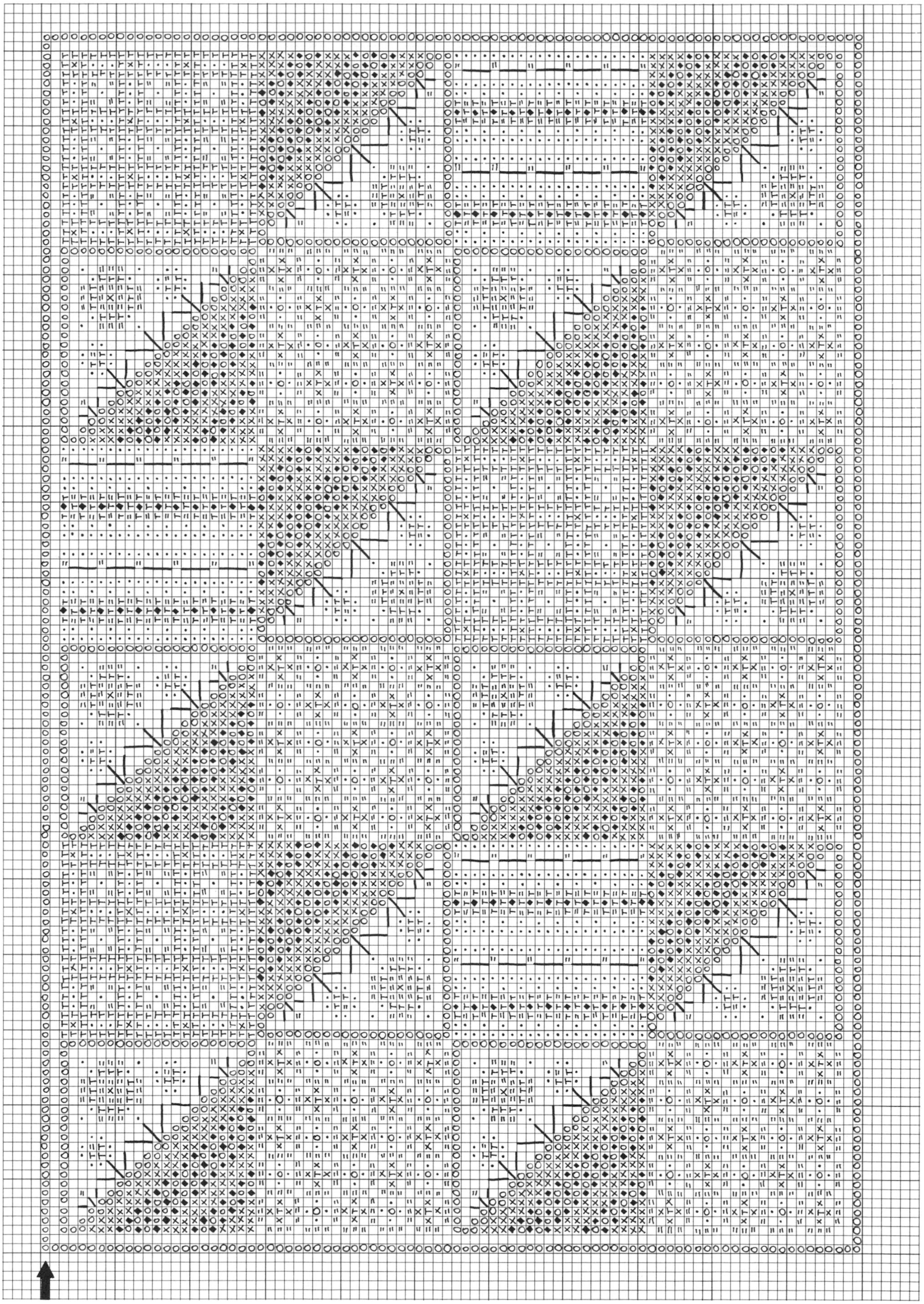

Dove

Size: Inset approximately 5⅛″ in diameter.

Perforated paper, 14-count, ivory: Cut paper 5¾″ square.

Embroidery floss: Coats 2302 Orange Lt. (or DMC 743), 2300 Burnt Orange (741), 2307 Christmas Gold (783), 7159 Blue Very Lt. (827), 2332 Burnt Orange Dk. (608), 6258 Willow Green (3345), 1001 White (Snow-White), 5371 Topaz Very Ultra Dk. (use Coats color), 7080 no name (798), and 5472 Coffee Brown Med. (801). Purchase one skein of each.

Other materials: Hand mirror by Sudberry House (white with 5″ round design area, outer dimensions 6″ × 12″, style #23302). Braided white rayon cording, ¼″ in diameter × ½ yard. Lightweight cardboard, 5¾″ square. Tracing paper, 7″ square. Sheet of white paper, 5¾″ square. White glue.

Making the first cross-stitch: Measure across 1⅞″ from top left corner; measure downwards 1″ from top left corner. Mark point where two measurements intersect. Start sewing at arrow.

Finishing directions

1. Remove and discard mounting board provided by Sudberry.
2. Carefully trace around circular edge of recessed design area on back of mirror. Fold circle in quarters. Open up. Cut out circle (Illus. 93).

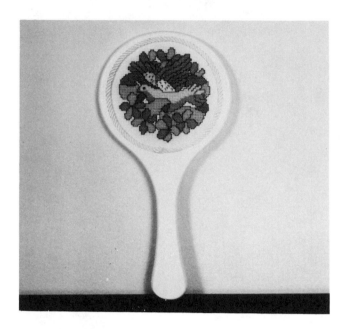

TRACING PAPER (R)

Illus. 93.

3. With paper pattern as guide and using a pencil, make one circle each of lightweight cardboard, white paper, and perforated paper. On perforated paper use folds in tracing paper to help center embroidery. Cut out circles.
4. Apply glue to back edges of cardboard. Press it inside design area. Let dry. With right sides up, repeat same procedure by stacking white paper and then embroidery in recess.

5. Glue white cording over edges of embroidery/white paper/cardboard. Start in middle of bottom; complete by butting ends together. As glue dries keep pressing braid into edges of design area (Illus. 94).

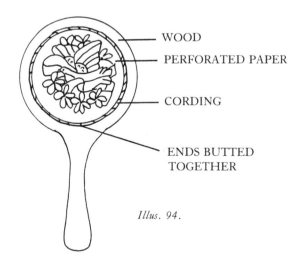

WOOD

PERFORATED PAPER

CORDING

ENDS BUTTED TOGETHER

Illus. 94.

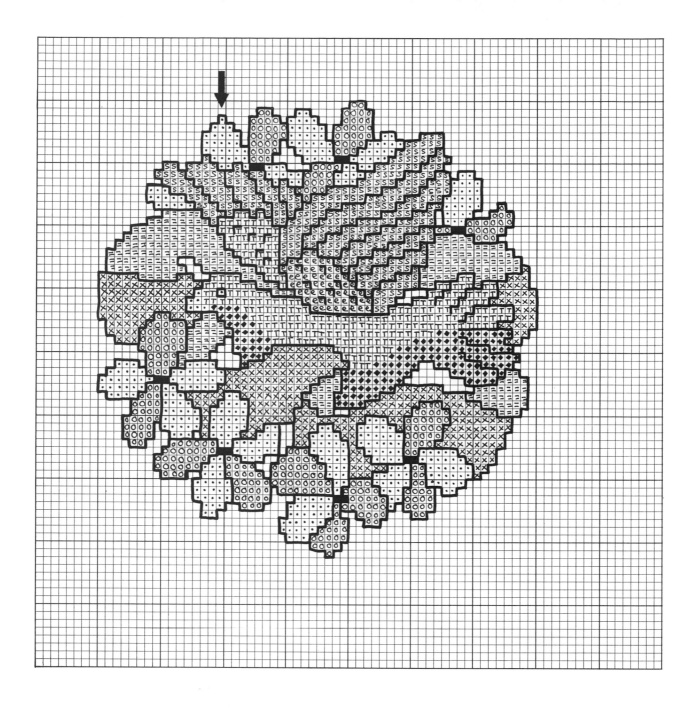

CROSS-STITCH COLOR KEY

Symbol	J. & P. Coats	DMC
T	2302 Orange Lt.	743
o	2300 Burnt Orange	741
◆	2307 Christmas Gold	783
⊠	7159 Blue Very Lt.	827
·	2332 Burnt Orange Dk.	608
■	6258 Willow Green	3345
e	1001 White	Snow-White
S	5371 Topaz Very Ultra Dk.	Use J. & P.
=	7080 no name	Coats color
☐	Fabric as is	798

BACKSTITCH COLOR KEY

Symbol	Area	J. & P. Coats	DMC
	All.	5472 Coffee Brown Med.	801

Horses *(In color, page F, Color Section I).*

Size: Aida square approximately 8½″ wide × 8.

Aida 11, ivory: Cut fabric 13″ wide × 12″.

Embroidery floss: Coats 6258 Willow Green (or DMC 987), 6001 Parrot Green Lt. (907), use DMC color (938), 5388 Beige (use Coats color), use DMC color (3046), use DMC color (611), 8403 Black (310), 6211 Jade Very Dk. (991), 6266 Apple Green (3348), 2326 Copper (920), 5000 Russet (436), use DMC color (414), 1001 White (Snow-White), 5470 no name (434), and 6226 Kelly Green (702). Purchase two skeins of 6266 Apple Green (3348). Buy one skein of each remaining color.

Other materials: Unfinished wooden plaque (10¼″ wide × 12¼″ × ¼ thick) (Illus. 95). Unbleached muslin, for lining, 11″ wide × 10″. White mat board, two pieces each measuring 10″ wide × 9″. Braided black nylon cording, 3/32″ in diameter × 1 yard. Sawtooth picture hanger. White glue.

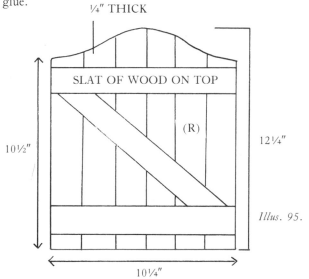

Illus. 95.

Making the first cross-stitch: Measure across 2½″ from top left corner; measure downwards 2½″ from top left corner. Mark point where two measurements intersect. Start sewing at arrow.

Finishing directions

1. Beyond embroidery add four blank squares of Aida on all four sides of design. Mark with pins. Using knotted single strand thread, hand-stitch these lines by following one row in Aida and by weaving in and out cloth with ½″ running stitches, pivoting at corners (Illus. 96).
2. Measure width and height of this newly stitched shape (mine is 8⅜″ wide × 7¾″). Cut two pieces of mat board, each measuring these dimensions.
3. Stack mat boards together. Tape in a north-south-east-west position.
4. Center muslin over mat boards. On back, fold in top and bottom. Tape. Fold in sides. Tape.

5. Repeat Steps 7–10 in "Mounting and Framing." The only exception is: At Step 7 there is no batting.
6. Glue black cording to edges of design. Start in middle of one side; curve first 1″ of cording back. Overlap ends by 1″; curve last 1″ of cording back (Illus. 97). As the glue dries, keep pressing cording onto the edges of Aida.
7. With right sides up, center and glue embroidery to wooden plaque. On back of design, spread glue in four corners. Put weight on top. Let dry.
8. On back of plaque, center sawtooth picture hanger along top edge.

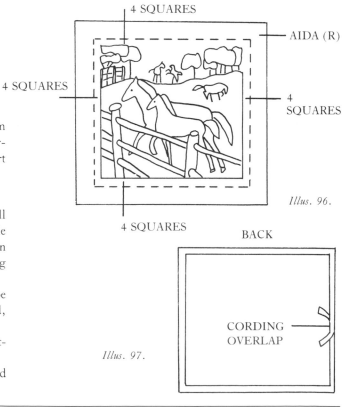

Illus. 96.

Illus. 97.

CROSS-STITCH COLOR KEY

Symbol	J. & P. Coats	DMC
◆	6258 Willow Green	987
③	6001 Parrot Green Lt.	907
⊠	Use DMC color	938
⊟	5388 Beige	Use J. & P. Coats color
○	Use DMC color	3046
⁄	Use DMC color	611
♥	8403 Black	310
Q	6211 Jade Very Dk.	991
·	6266 Apple Green	3348
L	2326 Copper	920
e	5000 Russet	436
U	Use DMC color	414
Z	1001 White	Snow-White
V	5470 no name	434
T	6226 Kelly Green	702
▢	Fabric as is	

BACKSTITCH COLOR KEY

Symbol	Area	J. & P. Coats	DMC
	All.	8403 Black	310

Single Ladies *(In color, page C, Color Section I)*.

Size: Runner approximately 13¼″ wide × 45″.

Aida 11, white: Cut fabric 13¼″ wide × 45″.

Embroidery floss: Coats 7080 no name (or DMC 798), 5470 no name (433), 2302 Orange Lt. (743), 2300 Burnt Orange (741), 2307 Christmas Gold (783), 7159 Blue Very Lt. (827), 2332 Burnt Orange Dk. (608), 6266 Apple Green (3348), 6258 Willow Green (3345), and 5387 Cream (Ecru). Purchase three skeins of 7159 Blue Very Lt. (827). Shop for two skeins of 7080 no name (798). Buy one skein of each remaining color.

Making the first cross-stitch: See Steps 2–5. Start sewing at arrows.

Finishing directions

1. Repeat fringing technique in Steps 1–3 in "Pennsylvania Dutch." The only exception is: At Step 1 measurement is ⅝″ (or seven Aida squares).

2. This runner has a centered design of two single rows of cross-stitches that surround one lady repeated at opposite ends of cloth. With runner held vertically, center 123 horizontal cross-stitches inside satin stitching. Starting in the lower left corner, count off 123 Aida squares. Mark end with pin. Count remaining squares to satin stitching at right (I had 14 squares, but this number could vary). Divide figure by two. Use resulting number to determine margins at sides and bottom of cloth (Illus. 98). Mark with pins. See arrow A on chart. Embroider 123 cross-stitches.

3. Turn runner upside down. Cross-stitch blue vertical lines coming out of stitches 1 and 123. Leave seven (this number could vary) blank squares of Aida at bottom of runner. Embroider 123 cross-stitches at this end of runner (Illus. 99).

4. Within first border, stitch second rectangle of blue cross-stitches.

5. See arrow B on chart. Embroider woman from top to bottom. Turn runner upside down. Repeat motif.

DETAIL OF BOTTOM OF RUNNER (R)

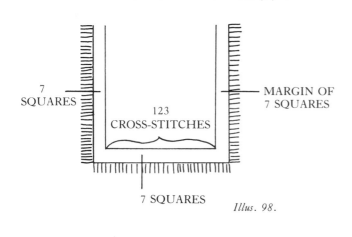

7 SQUARES

123 CROSS-STITCHES

MARGIN OF 7 SQUARES

7 SQUARES

Illus. 98.

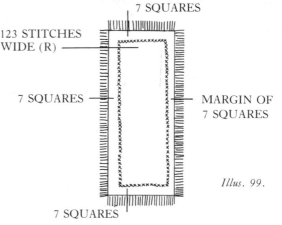

7 SQUARES

123 STITCHES WIDE (R)

7 SQUARES

MARGIN OF 7 SQUARES

7 SQUARES

Illus. 99.

CROSS-STITCH COLOR KEY

Symbol	J. & P. Coats	DMC
⊠	7080 *no name*	798
⊟	5470 *no name*	433
⊡	2302 *Orange Lt.*	743
③	2300 *Burnt Orange*	741
◆	2307 *Christmas Gold*	783
·	7159 *Blue Very Lt.*	827
■	2332 *Burnt Orange Dk.*	608
U	6266 *Apple Green*	3348
S	6258 *Willow Green*	3345
T	5387 *Cream*	Ecru
☐	*Fabric as is*	

BACKSTITCH COLOR KEY

Symbol	Area	J. & P. Coats	DMC
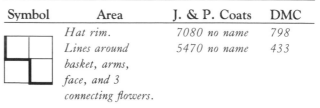	*Hat rim.*	7080 *no name*	798
	Lines around basket, arms, face, and 3 connecting flowers.	5470 *no name*	433

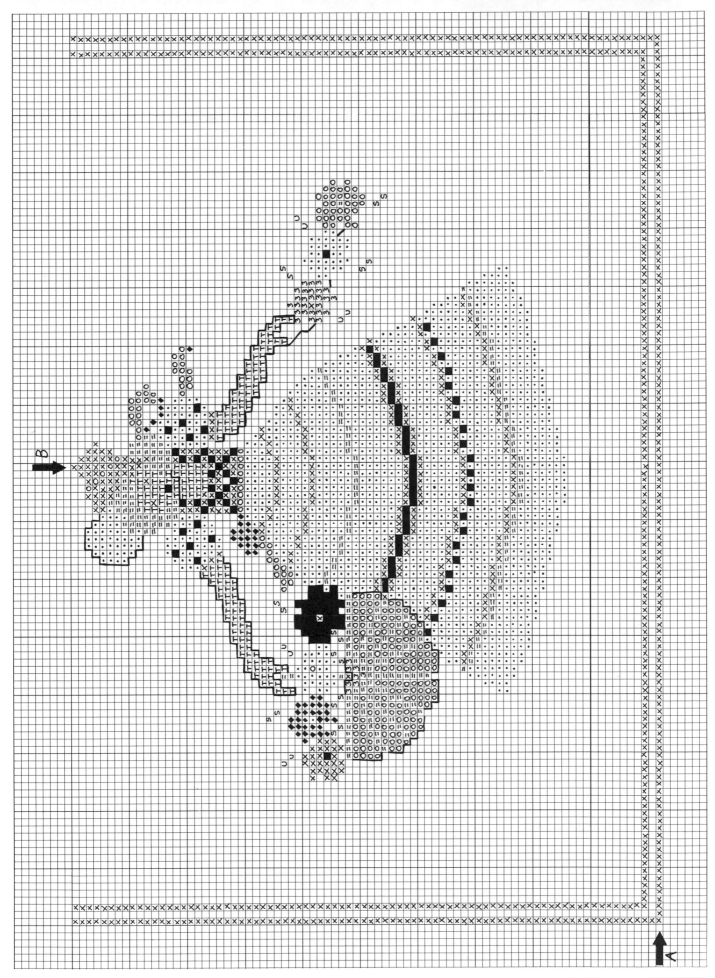

Growing and Cut Flowers *(In color, page F, Color Section I).*

Size: Band approximately 1⅞" wide × 38" without eyelet.

Maxi-weave riband, 14-count, white with blue edging, 1⅞" wide: Cut band 45".

Embroidery floss: Coats 7080 no name (or DMC 798), 2332 Burnt Orange Dk. (608), 2307 Christmas Gold (783), 7159 Blue Very Lt. (827), 6266 Apple Green (3348), 6258 Willow Green (3345), 5470 no name (433), 2302 Orange Lt. (743), and 2300 Burnt Orange (741). Purchase two skeins each of 5470 no name (433) and 2302 Orange Lt. (743). Buy one skein of each remaining color.

Other materials: Heavy basket, 38" around, just under top rim, 7½" high and 12½" in diameter (Illus. 100). White pre-gathered nylon eyelet edging, ⅞" wide × 2¼ yards.

Illus. 100.

Making the first cross-stitch: Measure across 3" from left end of horizontally held riband. Start sewing at arrow.

Finishing directions

1. Before doing embroidery, check basket measurement just under top rim. If your measurement is not 38", add or subtract embroidery. This design has two alternating repeats of one basket followed by three flowers. My band has 36¾" of embroidery, and each repeat is approximately 2½" wide. Towards end of design, keep trying riband on basket to make sure embroidery does not overlap.
2. Do embroidery.
3. Wash.
4. Finish off ends of Ribband. At start, fold fabric back just before embroidery. Press. Trim Ribband to 1" from fold. Place Ribband on basket; lap start over end. Cut end to 1½" beyond last embroidery (Illus. 101).
5. Stitch eyelet to top and bottom edges of Ribband. At start of eyelet, turn back ½". Press. With right sides up, place

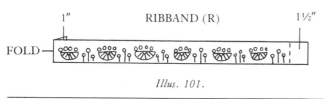

Illus. 101.

eyelet heading under blue edges of Ribband. Get beginning of eyelet even with left folded edge of Ribband. Pin. Baste. Cut trim same length as Ribband. Stitch just inside blue edging (Illus. 102).

6. Wrap Ribband around basket. Lap start over end. Pin. Slip-stitch.

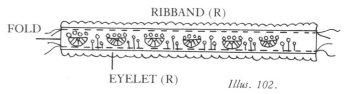

Illus. 102.

CROSS-STITCH COLOR KEY

Symbol	J. & P. Coats	DMC
⊠	7080 *no name*	798
■	2332 *Burnt Orange Dk.*	608
◆	2307 *Christmas Gold*	783
·	7159 *Blue Very Lt.*	827
U	6266 *Apple Green*	3348
S	6258 *Willow Green*	3345
=	5470 *no name*	433
O	2302 *Orange Lt.*	743
3	2300 *Burnt Orange*	741
☐	*Fabric as is*	

BACKSTITCH COLOR KEY

Symbol	Area	J. & P. Coats	DMC
	All.	5470 *no name*	433

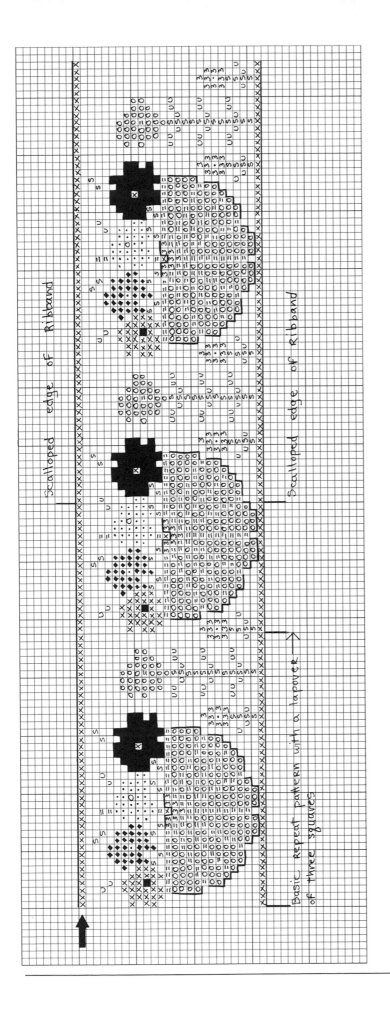

Scalloped edge of Ribband

Scalloped edge of Ribband

Basic Repeat pattern with a tapover of three squares

Onions, Squashes, and Pumpkin *(In color, page A, Color Section I).*

Size: Pillow approximately 12¼″ square without ruffle.

Background Aida, 14-count, ivory with rust threads: Cut fabric by Charles Craft 15″ square.

Embroidery floss: Coats 5371 Topaz Very Ultra Dk. (or DMC 436), 5471 Coffee Brown (801), 2326 Copper (920), 5363 Old Gold Lt. (729), 2292 Golden Yellow Very Lt. (3078), 5470 no name (433), 6211 Jade Very Dk. (367), use DMC color (890), 2327 Pumpkin Bright (970), 5365 no name (781), use DMC color (918), use DMC color (830), 5387 Cream (Ecru), 2293 Yellow Dark (743), 2307 Christmas Gold (783), 5472 Coffee Brown Med. (898), use DMC color (3047), 6001 Parrot Green Lt. (907), 2332 Burnt Orange Dk. (946), 5388 Beige (644), and 5478 Brown Very Ultra Dk. (3021). Purchase two skeins of 5470 no name (433). Buy one skein of each remaining color.

Other materials: Unbleached muslin, for back and ruffle, ⅞ yard. 12″ square pillow insert.

Making the first cross-stitch: Measure across 3¼″ from top left corner; measure downwards 3¼″ from top left corner. Mark point where two measurements intersect. Start sewing at arrow.

Finishing directions

1. Before doing embroidery, center of fabric must be prepared and unwoven. First, position cloth with rust threads running horizontally. With ruler and pins, mark off an 8½″ square in center of fabric. Using a knotted single strand of thread, hand-stitch these lines by following one row in Aida and by weaving in and out cloth with 1″ running stitches, pivoting at corners (Illus. 103).

FRONT VIEW

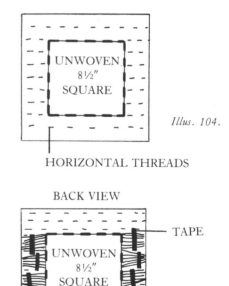

Illus. 104.

HORIZONTAL THREADS

BACK VIEW

Illus. 105.

BACKGROUND AIDA (R)

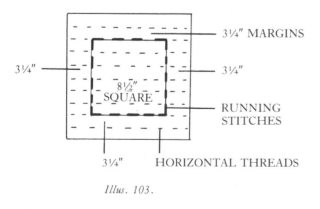

Illus. 103.

2. Within the 8½″ square, cut rust threads in half at middle. Then unweave the ends of each thread, one at a time, back to running stitches (Illus. 104). Use transparent tape on the ends of threads to keep them in groups on the back of Aida (Illus. 105).
3. Do embroidery.

4. After embroidery is finished, remove transparent tape groupings one cluster at a time. Rethread each rust thread, and weave back into untouched portions of rust lines. At edges of cloth, cut rust threads even with fabric (Illus. 106).
5. Wash.
6. Make pillow patterns for front (Illus. 107) and back (Illus. 108).
7. With right sides up, lay front pattern over embroidery. Center design (margins should be about 2″ on all sides). Pin. Cut. Transfer stitching lines to wrong side front.
8. Lay out and cut back. Transfer stitching lines and dots to wrong side.

BACK VIEW DETAIL, RIGHT SIDE REWOVEN

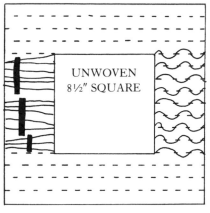

UNWOVEN
8½″ SQUARE

Illus. 106.

FRONT: CUT ONE, EMBROIDERED AIDA

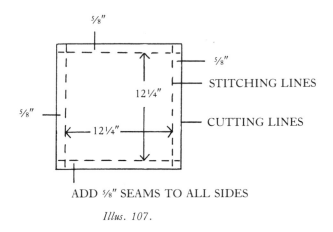

⅝″

⅝″ — STITCHING LINES

12¼″

⅝″

12¼″ — CUTTING LINES

ADD ⅝″ SEAMS TO ALL SIDES

Illus. 107.

BACK: CUT TWO, UNBLEACHED MUSLIN

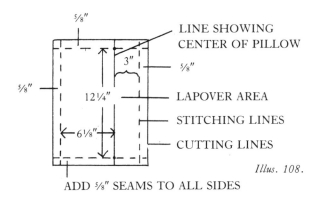

⅝″

LINE SHOWING
CENTER OF PILLOW

3″

⅝″

⅝″

12¼″ — LAPOVER AREA

STITCHING LINES

6⅛″

CUTTING LINES

Illus. 108.

ADD ⅝″ SEAMS TO ALL SIDES

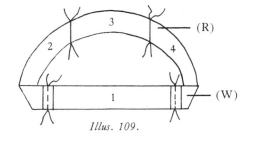

3

2   4 — (R)

1 — (W)

Illus. 109.

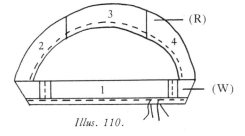

3

(R)

2   4

1 — (W)

Illus. 110.

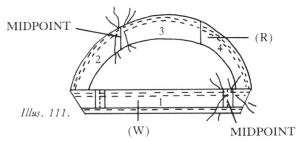

MIDPOINT

3   (R)

2   4

Illus. 111.

1

(W)   MIDPOINT

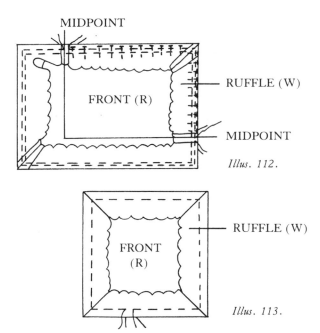

MIDPOINT

FRONT (R) — RUFFLE (W)

MIDPOINT

Illus. 112.

FRONT
(R) — RUFFLE (W)

Illus. 113.

9. For ruffle, cut four strips of fabric each 4″ wide and 36″ long.

10. With right sides together, stitch four ruffle sections. Make ½″ seams, and press open (Illus. 109).

11. Narrow-hem the bottom of ruffle. To do so, turn up ½″ seam allowance on lower edge. Press. Pin. Stitch close to inner edge (Illus. 110).

12. Gather top of ruffle. First, divide ruffle in half by starting at one seam and marking the midway point at opposite seam. Stitch ½″ from upper edges using long machine-stitches, breaking at midpoints. Stitch again ¼″ away in seam allowances (Illus. 111).

13. With right sides together, put half-ruffle on front. Start by placing one seam in upper left corner and halfway point at the lower right corner. Get ½″ stitching line on ruffle to rest on the stitching lines transferred to wrong side front. Evenly adjust gathers. Pin (Illus. 112).

Charts and color keys on pages 96 and 97.

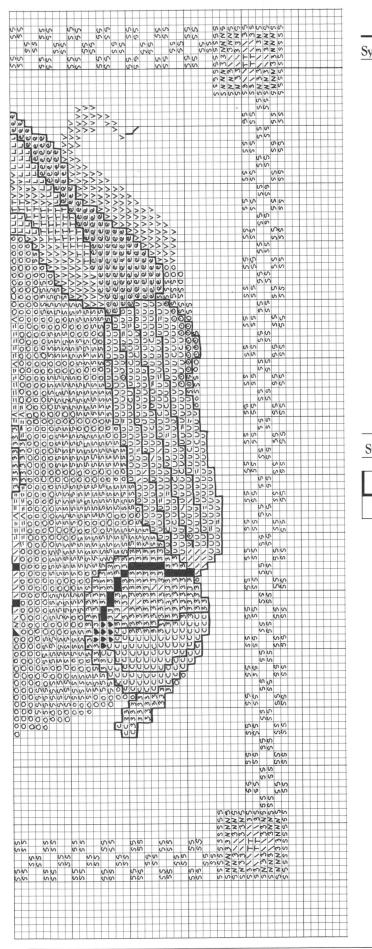

CROSS-STITCH COLOR KEY

Symbol	J. & P. Coats	DMC
⊡	5371 Topaz Very Ultra Dk.	436
⊠	5471 Coffee Brown	801
③	2326 Copper	920
©	5363 Old Gold Lt.	729
⧄	2292 Golden Yellow Very Lt.	3078
Ⓢ	5470 no name	433
Ⓝ	6211 Jade Very Dk.	367
◿	Use DMC color	890
⊟	2327 Pumpkin Bright	970
◆	5365 no name	781
Ⓤ	Use DMC color	918
Ⓥ	Use DMC color	830
⊙	5387 Cream	Ecru
Ⓛ	2293 Yellow Dark	743
Ⓣ	2307 Christmas Gold	783
♥	5472 Coffee Brown Med.	898
⒠	Use DMC color	3047
■	6001 Parrot Green Lt.	907
⟋⟍	2332 Burnt Orange Dk.	946
·	5388 Beige	644
☐	Fabric as is	

BACKSTITCH COLOR KEY

Symbol	Area	J. & P. Coats	DMC
	Outlines around and within 3 corns.	5478 Brown Very Ultra Dk.	3021
	Lines at top of both butternut squash and outlines around and within 3 onions.	6001 Parrot Green Lt.	907
	Short individual lines within acorn squash.	6211 Jade Very Dk.	367
	Single line at bottom of left butternut squash.	5365 no name	781
	Short lines at end of bottom left onion.	5472 Coffee Brown Med.	898
	Short lines at end of upper right onion.	5470 no name	433
	Outline and tips around ends of corn husks which are cross-stitched in 2307 Christmas Gold.	2307 Christmas Gold	783
	Two lines on bottom corn husk that border on the DMC color 830.	2293 Yellow Dark	743
	Tips and lines around and within 3 corn husks.	Use DMC color	830

14. Gather and pin remaining half-ruffle on front.

15. Stitch ruffle to front, pivoting at corners (Illus. 113).

16. On back sections, turn in center edge along seam line. Press. Turn under ¼″ on raw edge. Press. Pin. Stitch close to inner edge (Illus. 114).

17. With right sides down, pin the left back on the right back, matching large ●'s. Stitch across lapover area (Illus. 115).

18. With right sides together, pin front on back. Stitch, pivoting at corners. Trim seams to ½″ (Illus. 116).

19. Turn. Push insert through slit in pillow back.

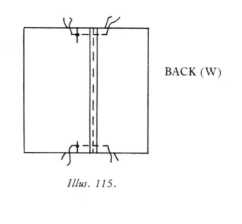

BACK (W)

Illus. 115.

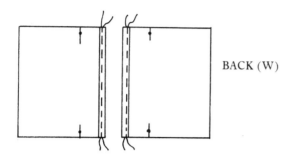

BACK (W)

Illus. 114.

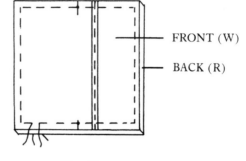

 FRONT (W)

BACK (R)

Illus. 116.

CHALLENGING
PROJECTS

Fruit Basket *(In color, page G, Color Section I).*

Size: Pillow approximately 12¼″ square without ruffle.

Hopscotch, 14-count Aida, rust and ivory combination: Cut fabric by Charles Craft 15″ square.

Embroidery floss: Coats 3046 Christmas Red Bright (or DMC 666), 3000 Garnet (304), 2288 Lemon Lt. (445), 6256 Parrot Green Med. (906), 5472 Coffee Brown Med. (898), 7080 no name (798), use DMC color (775), 7981 Navy Blue (791), 2326 Copper (920), 7159 Blue Very Lt. (827), 5371 Topaz Very Ultra Dk. (436), 3335 Sportsman Flesh (945), 6205 Emerald Green Med. (911), 6001 Parrot Green Lt. (907), 6267 Avocado Green (469), 5470 no name (433), 2302 Orange Lt. (743), 2307 Christmas Gold (783), 2327 Pumpkin Bright (970), and 2332 Burnt Orange Dk. (946). Purchase one skein of each.

Other materials: Rust and ivory cotton print, for back and ruffle, ¾ yard. 12″ square pillow insert.

Making the first cross-stitch: See Step 1.

Finishing directions

1. Embroider only in solid areas of cloth. Start embroidery in top left corner of Hopscotch. From bottom of rust square and on right side, count up 21 vertical squares on Aida. At square 21, count 13 horizontal squares to left. At point where these two measurements intersect (Illus. 117), start sewing at arrow. Sew entire corner. Then move to solid ivory center.

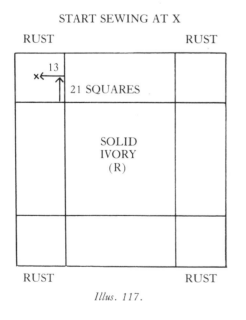

START SEWING AT X

Illus. 117.

2. Repeat Steps 5–8 in "Onions, Squashes, and Pumpkin."
3. For ruffle, cut three strips of fabric each 4″ wide and 44″ long.
4. Repeat Steps 10–19 in "Onions, Squashes, and Pumpkin." The only exception is: At Step 10 there are three strips of ruffle.

CROSS-STITCH COLOR KEY

Symbol	J. & P. Coats	DMC
Z	3046 *Christmas Red Bright*	666
ɜ	3000 *Garnet*	304
■	2288 *Lemon Lt.*	445
□	6256 *Parrot Green Med.*	906
△	5472 *Coffee Brown Med.*	898
=	7080 *no name*	798
◆	*Use DMC color*	775
T	7981 *Navy Blue*	791
◪	2326 *Copper*	920
e	7159 *Blue Very Lt.*	827
⊠	5371 *Topaz Very Ultra Dk.*	436
·	3335 *Sportsman Flesh*	945
C	6205 *Emerald Green Med.*	911
U	6001 *Parrot Green Lt.*	907
R	6267 *Avocado Green*	469
V	5470 *no name*	433
Z	2302 *Orange Lt.*	743
L	2307 *Christmas Gold*	783
◩	2327 *Pumpkin Bright*	970
N	2332 *Burnt Orange Dk.*	946
□	*Fabric as is*	

BACKSTITCH COLOR KEY

Symbol	Area	J. & P. Coats	DMC
	Outline around leaves; grape stems; basket handle; and all lines around and within basket.	5472 Coffee Brown Med.	898
	Outline around pear.	6267 Avocado Green	469
	Stems connecting bottom leaves.	6205 Emerald Green Med.	911

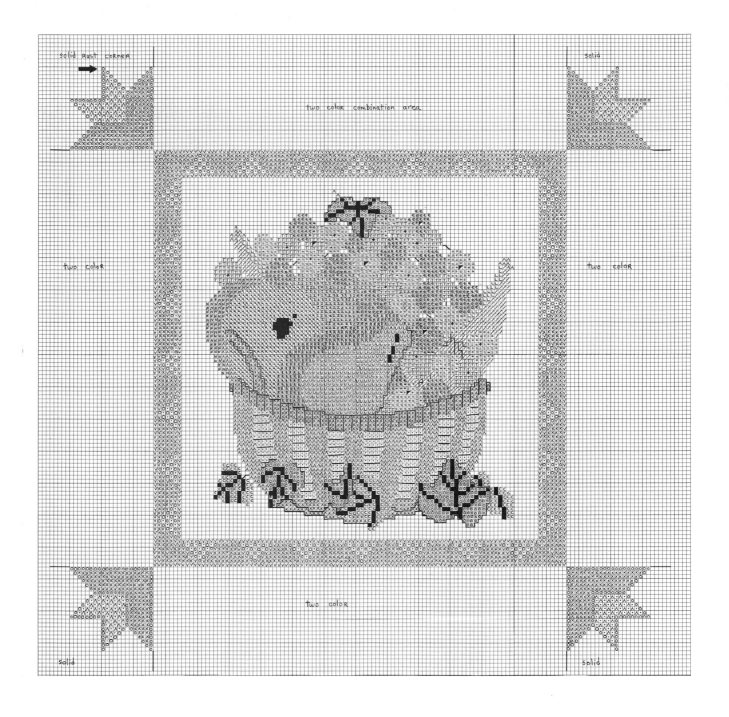

Cut Apple with Other Fruits *(In color, page L, Color Section II)*.

Size: Pillow approximately 12¼" square without ruffle.

Background Aida, 14-count, ivory with rust threads: Cut fabric by Charles Craft 15" square.

Embroidery floss: Coats 5371 Topaz Very Ultra Dk. (or DMC 436), 5470 no name (433), 5472 Coffee Brown Med. (898), 7159 Blue Very Lt. (827), 7080 no name (798), 7981 Navy Blue (791), use DMC color (775), 2326 Copper (920), 2327 Pumpkin Bright (970), 2332 Burnt Orange Dk. (946), 2292 Golden Yellow Very Lt. (3078), 2290 Canary Bright (973), 5363 Old Gold Lt. (729), 6001 Parrot Green Lt. (907), 6267 Avocado Green (469), use DMC color (369), 6239 Parrot Green Dk. (702), 2302 Orange Lt. (743), 2307 Christmas Gold (783), 5478 Brown Very Ultra Dk. (3021), 3046 Christmas Red Bright (666), 3000 Garnet (304), and 5388 Beige (3033). Purchase two skeins each of 5470 no name (433) and 2326 Copper (920). Buy one skein of each remaining color.

Other materials: Rust cotton, for back and ruffle, ¾ yard. 12" square pillow insert.

Making the first cross-stitch: Measure across 3⅛" from top left corner; measure downwards 3⅛" from top left corner. Mark point where two measurements intersect. Start sewing at arrow.

Finishing directions

1. Before doing embroidery, center of fabric must be prepared and unwoven. First, position cloth with rust threads running vertically. Then refer above to first two sentences in "Making the first cross-stitch." At point marked with pin, count off 122 Aida squares to right (horizontally) and 122 Aida squares to bottom (vertically) (Illus. 118). Mark ends with pins. Using knotted single strand of thread, hand-stitch outline of square by following one row in Aida and by weaving in and out cloth with 1" running stitches (Illus. 119).

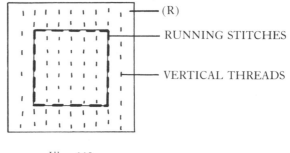

Illus. 119.

2. Repeat Steps 2–8 in "Onions, Squashes, and Pumpkin." The only exception is: At Step 2 these rust threads are vertically positioned.

3. For ruffle, cut three strips of fabric each 4" wide and 44" long.

4. Repeat Steps 10–19 in "Onions, Squashes, and Pumpkin." The only exception is: At Step 10 there are three strips of ruffle.

BACKGROUND AIDA (R)

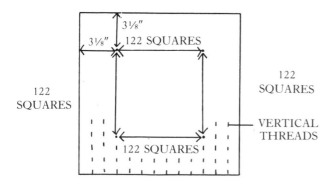

Illus. 118.

CROSS-STITCH COLOR KEY

Symbol	J. & P. Coats	DMC
S	5371 Topaz Very Ultra Dk.	436
·	5470 no name	433
◆	5472 Coffee Brown Med.	898
T	7159 Blue Very Lt.	827
e	7080 no name	798
L	7981 Navy Blue	791
◪	Use DMC color	775
⊠	2326 Copper	920
R	2327 Pumpkin Bright	970
U	2332 Burnt Orange Dk.	946
△	2292 Golden Yellow Very Lt.	3078
P	2290 Canary Bright	973
N	5363 Old Gold Lt.	729
Z	6001 Parrot Green Lt.	907
≡	6267 Avocado Green	469
♥	Use DMC color	369
❚	6239 Parrot Green Dk.	702
○	2302 Orange Lt.	743
▢	2307 Christmas Gold	783
■	5478 Brown Very Ultra Dk.	3021
3	3046 Christmas Red Bright	666
◣	3000 Garnet	304
C	5388 Beige	3033
□	Fabric as is	

BACKSTITCH COLOR KEY

Symbol	Area	J. & P. Coats	DMC
	Outline around apple slice.	3000 Garnet	304
	Line down center of slice and whole apple.	5363 Old Gold Lt.	729
	Grape stems; outline around handle, sides, bottom, and within basket; and short horizontal lines suggesting a tablecloth.	5470 no name	433
	Squares within the repeat border and lines around 3 staples on basket rim.	2326 Copper	920
	Outline around grape.	7080 no name	798

Chart on page 104.

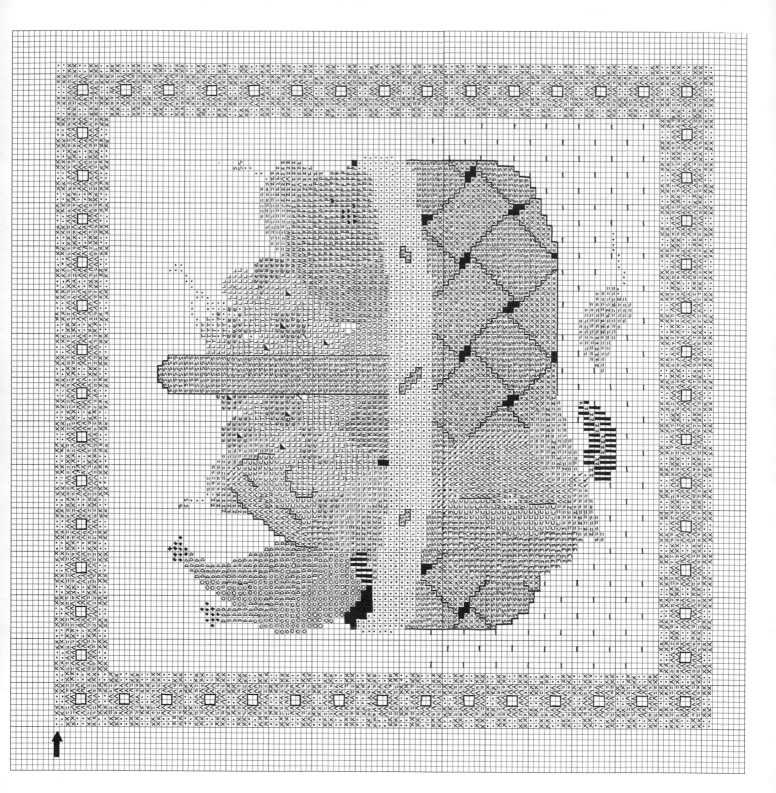

Framed Basket *(In color, page M, Color Section II).*

Size: Embroidery approximately 9½″ wide × 10½″ without edging.

Fiddler's Cloth, 14-count, oatmeal: Cut fabric by Charles Craft 15″ wide × 12″.

Embroidery floss: Coats 2290 Canary Bright (or DMC 973), 6020 Nile Green (955), 3151 Cranberry Very Lt. (3326), 3067 Baby Pink (818), 3153 Geranium (956), 3065 Cranberry Very Dk. (601), use DMC color (890), 5470 no name (433), 6256 Parrot Green Med. (906), use DMC color (472), 6211 Jade Very Dk. (991), 6258 Willow Green (3345), 6266 Apple Green (3348), use DMC color (3045), 2293 Yellow Dark (744), 2308 Golden Brown Med. (977), use DMC color (610), and 3046 Christmas Red Bright (666). Purchase two skeins each of 5470 no name (433), use DMC color (472), and 6266 Apple Green (3348). Buy one skein of each remaining color.

Other materials: Premade corduroy bedrest in beige. Flat ivory crochet edging, 1″ wide × 1¼ yards.

Making the first cross-stitch: Measure across 2½″ from top left corner; measure downwards 1″ from top left corner. Mark point where two measurements intersect. Start sewing at arrow.

Finishing directions

1. With right sides up, add ⅜″ margins beyond all four sides of design. Mark with pins. Using knotted single strand of thread, hand-stitch these lines by following one row in fabric and by weaving in and out cloth with 1″ running stitches (Illus. 120).

2. On running stitch lines, fold edges of Fiddler's Cloth towards wrong side fabric. Press sides first, then top and bottom. Cut fabric beyond running stitches to ½″ seam allowances.

3. With right sides up, add trim to edges of embroidered cloth. Start in middle of bottom, and turn back end ¼″. Baste so top ³⁄₁₆″ of trim rests under folded edges of cloth; ease around corners. Overlap ends by 1½″. Turn back end ¼″. Stitch ⅛″ from folded edges of cloth, pivoting at corners (Illus. 121).

4. Center embroidery on bedrest. Pin. Baste back of Fiddler's Cloth to corduroy; do not attach by trim.

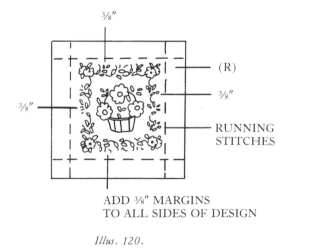

ADD ⅜″ MARGINS
TO ALL SIDES OF DESIGN

Illus. 120.

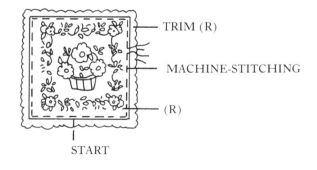

TRIM (R)

MACHINE-STITCHING

(R)

START

Illus. 121.

Chart and color key on pages 106 and 107.

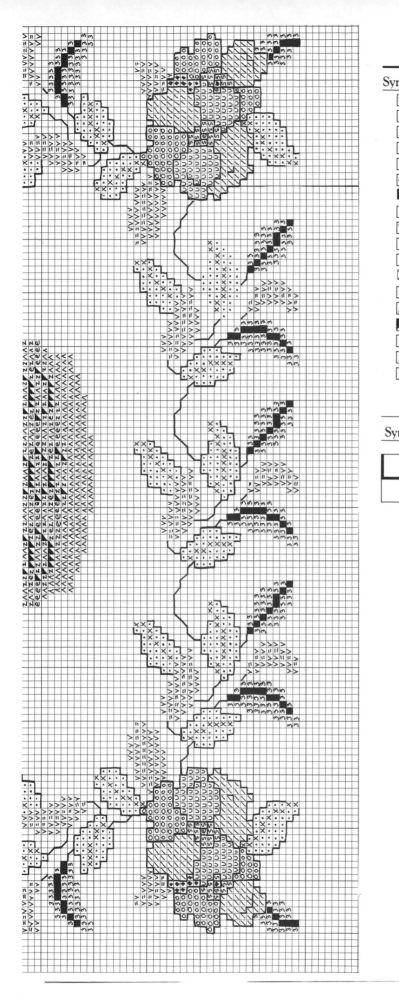

CROSS-STITCH COLOR KEY

Symbol	J. & P. Coats	DMC
♥	2290 Canary Bright	973
S	6020 Nile Green	955
∕	3151 Cranberry Very Lt.	3326
U	3067 Baby Pink	818
○	3153 Geranium	956
◆	3065 Cranberry Very Dk.	601
■	Use DMC color	890
T	5470 no name	433
V	6256 Parrot Green Med.	906
·	Use DMC color	472
=	6211 Jade Very Dk.	991
⊠	6258 Willow Green	3345
3	6266 Apple Green	3348
∧	Use DMC color	3045
◢	2293 Yellow Dark	744
e	2308 Golden Brown Med.	977
Z	Use DMC color	610
□	Fabric as is	

BACKSTITCH COLOR KEY

Symbol	Area	J. & P. Coats	DMC
	Center of each flower.	3046 Christmas Red Bright	666
	All stems and the outlines around and within the petals of each flower.	5470 no name	433
	The outlines around the lightest leaves.	6258 Willow Green	3345

Welcome *(In color, page I, Color Section II)*.

Size: Embroidery approximately 8½" in diameter.

Aida 11, white: Cut fabric 14½" square.

Embroidery floss: Coats 8403 Black (or DMC 310), 1001 White (Snow-White), 3281 Pink Med. (use Coats color), 8401 Steel Grey (use Coats color), use DMC color (317), 3000 Garnet (309), 6001 Parrot Green Lt. (907), 7080 no name (use Coats color), use DMC color (761), 5371 Topaz Very Ultra Dk. (437), 6226 Kelly Green (702), 5471 Coffee Brown (433), use DMC color (3371), 6020 Nile Green (955), use DMC color (890), and use DMC color (3045). Purchase two skeins of 3281 Pink Med. (use Coats color). Buy one skein of each remaining color.

Other materials: White wicker wreath by Crafts Home Decor, 13" wide × 1¾" thick with design area of 10" in diameter (Illus. 122). Bleached muslin, for backing, 14" square. Stitch Witchery, 14" square. White mat board, 14" square. Blue grosgrain ribbon, ⅜" wide × 3½ yards. Tracing paper, 15" square. One white cloth-covered tie wire, 18". Compass. White glue.

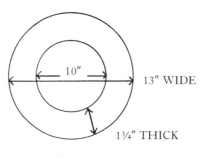

Illus. 122.

Making the first cross-stitch: Measure across 6½" from top left corner; measure downwards 3" from top left corner. Mark point where two measurements intersect. Start sewing at arrow.

Finishing directions
1. Repeat Step 1 in "Strawberries."
2. With right sides up, place wreath over tracing paper. Trace around outer and inner edges. Divide circle into four

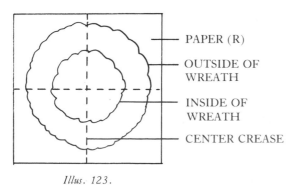

Illus. 123.

equal quarters by folding and creasing. Open up paper (Illus. 123).

3. With right sides up on tracing paper and using a compass, redraw outer circle. Then draw a second circle ½" to inside (Illus. 124). The edges of this inner circle will be your pattern for cutting Aida and mat board to size.

4. With right sides up, place paper circle over Aida combination. Use quarter segments in circle as guidelines to center paper over embroidery. Pin. Cut Aida combination and mat board to size of inner circle.

5. With right sides up, glue Aida combination to mat board. Spread glue ½" from outer edges mat board. Put weight on top. Let dry.

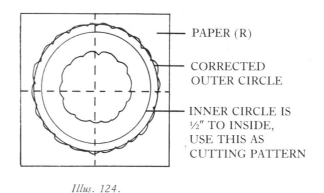

Illus. 124.

6. Cut grosgrain into two pieces measuring 1¼ and 2¼ yards.
7. With 2¼-yard length, wrap ribbon around wreath. Double-knot ends at top back (Illus. 125).

BACK

Illus. 125.

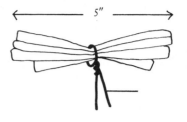

Illus. 126.

8. With 1¼-yard length, make bow. Loop ribbon back and forth between 5″ width. With white tie wire, wrap center of bow and tightly twist it several times on back (Illus. 126).
9. With right sides up, center bow over top of wreath. Slip wire ends through to back of wreath; twist ends together. With wire end, make ½″ circular loop to hang project on wall. Tuck wire end into wreath (Illus. 127).
10. With right sides up, center and glue wreath over Aida combination. Spread glue ½″ from outer edges of Aida. Put weight on top. Let dry. All edges of wreath may not touch Aida.

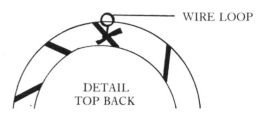

WIRE LOOP

DETAIL
TOP BACK

Illus. 127.

CROSS-STITCH COLOR KEY

Symbol	J. & P. Coats	DMC
e	8403 Black	310
U	1001 White	Snow-White
⊠	3281 Pink Med.	Use J. & P. Coats color
T	8401 Steel Grey	Use J. & P. Coats color
S	Use DMC color	317
♥	3000 Garnet	309
■	6001 Parrot Green Lt.	907
Z	7080 no name	Use J. & P. Coats color
Q	Use DMC color	761
O	5371 Topaz Very Ultra Dk.	437
△	6226 Kelly Green	702
=	5471 Coffee Brown	433
◆	Use DMC color	3371
·	6020 Nile Green	955
╱	Use DMC color	890
3	Use DMC color	3045
☐	Fabric as is	

BACKSTITCH COLOR KEY

Symbol	Area	J. & P. Coats	DMC
	Vines on tree at right.	3000 Garnet	309
	All other areas.	8403 Black	310

Chart and color key on page 110.

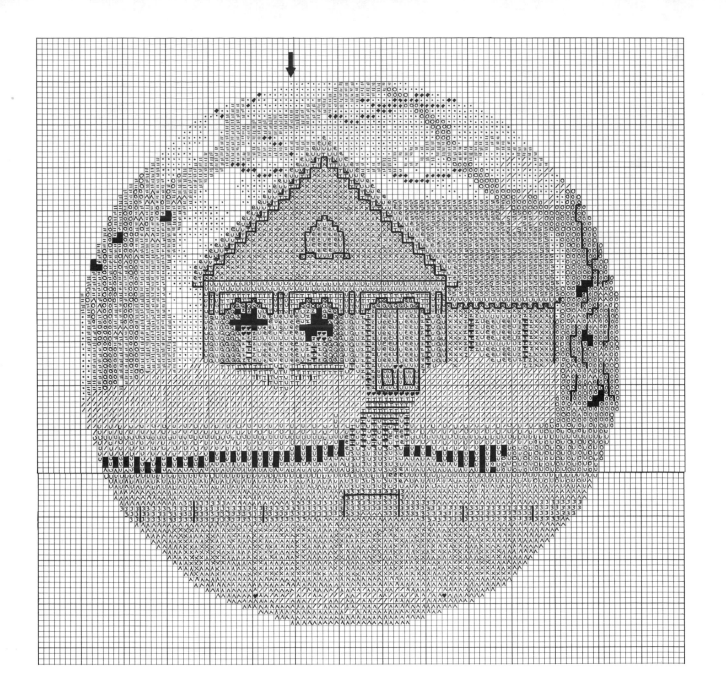

Come Live with Me *(In color, page H, Color Section I)*.

Quote: *The Passionate Shepherd to His Love.* Christopher Marlowe.

Size: Wall hanging approximately 15½″ wide × 17″.

Aida 11, ivory: Cut fabric 20″ wide × 21″.

Embroidery floss: Coats 6228 Christmas Green (or DMC 699), 6239 Parrot Green Dk. (702), use DMC color (471), 2334 Bright Orange Red (606), 2300 Burnt Orange (740), 5472 Coffee Brown Med. (801), 7010 Imperial Blue (use Coats color), 3021 Christmas Red Dk. (816), 6001 Parrot Green Lt. (907), 2302 Orange Lt. (743), 3011 Coral (351), 5000 Russet (435), 1001 White (Snow-White), 8403 Black (310), 8401 Steel Grey (318), 5363 Old Gold Lt. (use Coats color), 6020 Nile Green (966), 5387 Cream (Ecru), 6267 Avocado Green (469), and 8397 no name (762). Purchase two skeins each of 6228 Christmas Green (699), 6239 Parrot Green Dk. (702), use DMC color (471), 5472 Coffee Brown Med. (801), and 5000 Russet (435). Buy one skein of each remaining color.

Making the first cross-stitch: Measure across 3¼″ from top left corner; measure downwards 3″ from top left corner. Mark point where two measurements intersect. Start sewing at arrow.

Finishing directions
1. See "Mounting and Framing."
2. Margin to be added at mounting: Add 1″.

Chart and color key on pages 112 and 113.

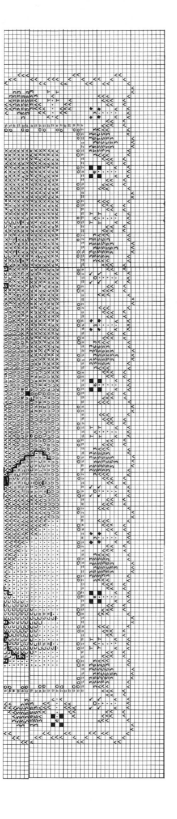

CROSS-STITCH COLOR KEY

Symbol	J. & P. Coats	DMC
△	6228 Christmas Green	699
⊠	6239 Parrot Green Dk.	702
·	Use DMC color	471
■	2334 Bright Orange Red	606
e	2300 Burnt Orange	740
o	5472 Coffee Brown Med.	801
◆	7010 Imperial Blue	Use J. & P. Coats color
3	3021 Christmas Red Dk.	816
N	6001 Parrot Green Lt.	907
S	2302 Orange Lt.	743
T	3011 Coral	351
=	5000 Russet	435
N	1001 White	Snow-White
♥	8403 Black	310
L	8401 Steel Grey	318
⟍	5363 Old Gold Lt.	Use J. & P. Coats color
Z	6020 Nile Green	966
C	5387 Cream	Ecru
U	6267 Avocado Green	469
V	8397 no name	762
□	Fabric as is	

BACKSTITCH COLOR KEY

Symbol	Area	J. & P. Coats	DMC
⌐	Outline on sides of house and line between roof and top of house.	3021 Christmas Red Dk.	816
	All other outlines and details on birds, trees, house, lambs, and dog.	8403 Black	310

Flowers and Lace *(In color, page L, Color Section II).*

Size: Each embroidery approximately 13¾″ square.

Aida 8, white: Cut two rectangles each 30″ wide × 24″.

Embroidery floss: Coats 7080 no name (or DMC 798), 5470 no name (433), 2302 Orange Lt. (743), 2300 Burnt Orange (741), 2307 Christmas Gold (783), 7159 Blue Very Lt. (827), 2332 Burnt Orange Dk. (608), 6266 Apple Green (3348), 6258 Willow Green (3345), and 1001 White (Snow-White). Purchase twelve skeins of 7080 no name (798) and three skeins each of 2307 Christmas Gold (783) and 7159 Blue Very Lt. (827). Shop for two skeins each of 5470 no name (433), 2302 Orange Lt. (743), and 6266 Apple Green (3348). Buy one skein of each remaining color.

Other materials: White cotton, for ruffle, 1½ yards. Medium-weight white cotton, for back, 1 yard. Two standard pillows, 26″ wide × 20″.

Making the first cross-stitch: On each fabric measure across 8″ from top left corner; measure downwards 4¾″ from top left corner. Mark point where two measurements intersect. Start sewing at arrow.

Finishing directions

1. With right sides up, add 6¼″ margins on sides and 3″ margins at top and bottom. Measure from tops of blue lace. Mark with pins. Using knotted single strand of white thread, hand-stitch these lines by following one row in Aida and by weaving in and out cloth with 1″ running stitches. Check to see that dimensions within these stitches are 26″ wide × 20″ (Illus. 128). These running stitches will later be your markings for matching fabrics and machine-stitching.

2. Make pillow pattern for back (Illus. 129).
3. Layout and cut back. Transfer stitching lines and dots to the wrong side of the fabric.
4. For ruffle on each sham, cut six strips of fabric each 4″ wide and 44″ long.
5. Repeat Steps 10–18 in "Onions, Squashes, and Pumpkin." The only exceptions are: At Step 10 there are six strips of ruffle, and; that you are making two shams.
6. Turn. Push standard pillow through slit in sham back.

BACK: CUT FOUR, WHITE COTTON

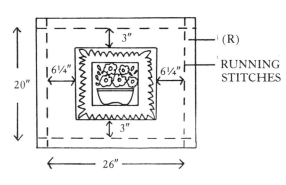

Illus. 128.

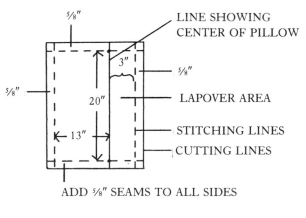

ADD ⅝″ SEAMS TO ALL SIDES

Illus. 129.

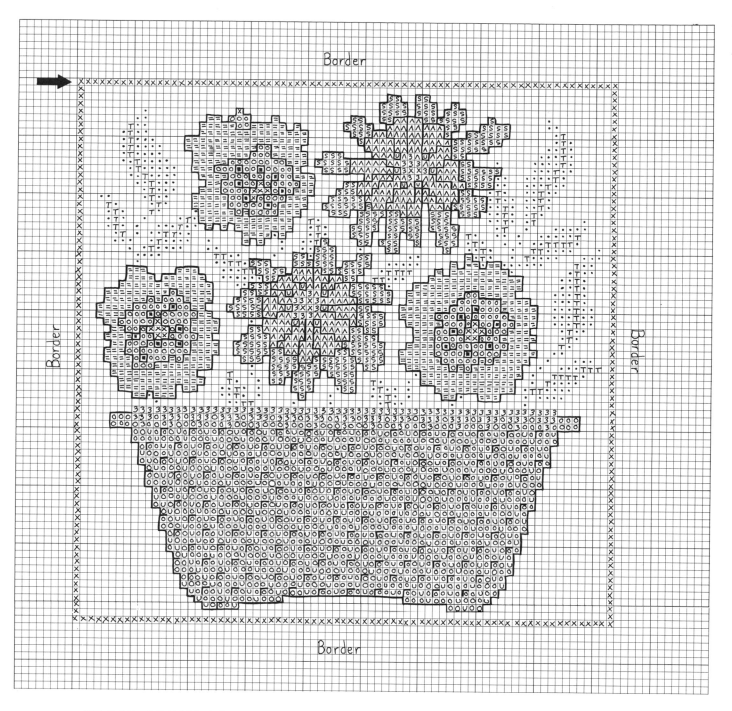

CROSS-STITCH COLOR KEY

Symbol	J. & P. Coats	DMC
⊠	7080 no name	798
3	5470 no name	433
S	2302 Orange Lt.	743
△	2300 Burnt Orange	741
≡	2307 Christmas Gold	783
○	7159 Blue Very Lt.	827
■	2332 Burnt Orange Dk.	608
·	6266 Apple Green	3348
T	6258 Willow Green	3345
U	1001 White	Snow-White
☐	Fabric as is	

BACKSTITCH COLOR KEY

Symbol	Area	J. & P. Coats	DMC
	Single lines within decorative lace.	7080 no name	798
	Lines around and within flowers and basket.	5470 no name	433

Chart for other pillowcase is on pages 116 and 117. Use same instructions for both borders that are given in this chart.

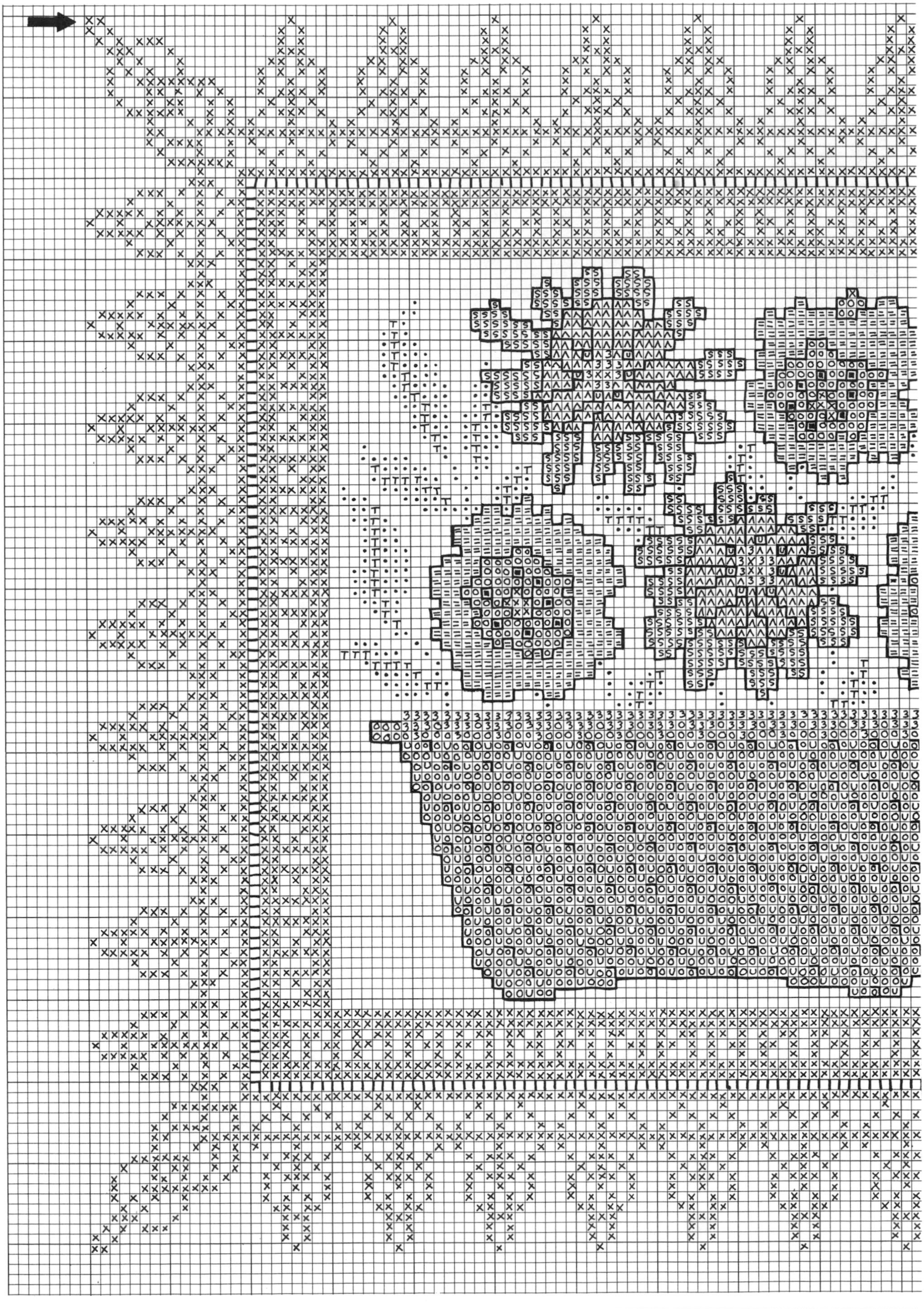

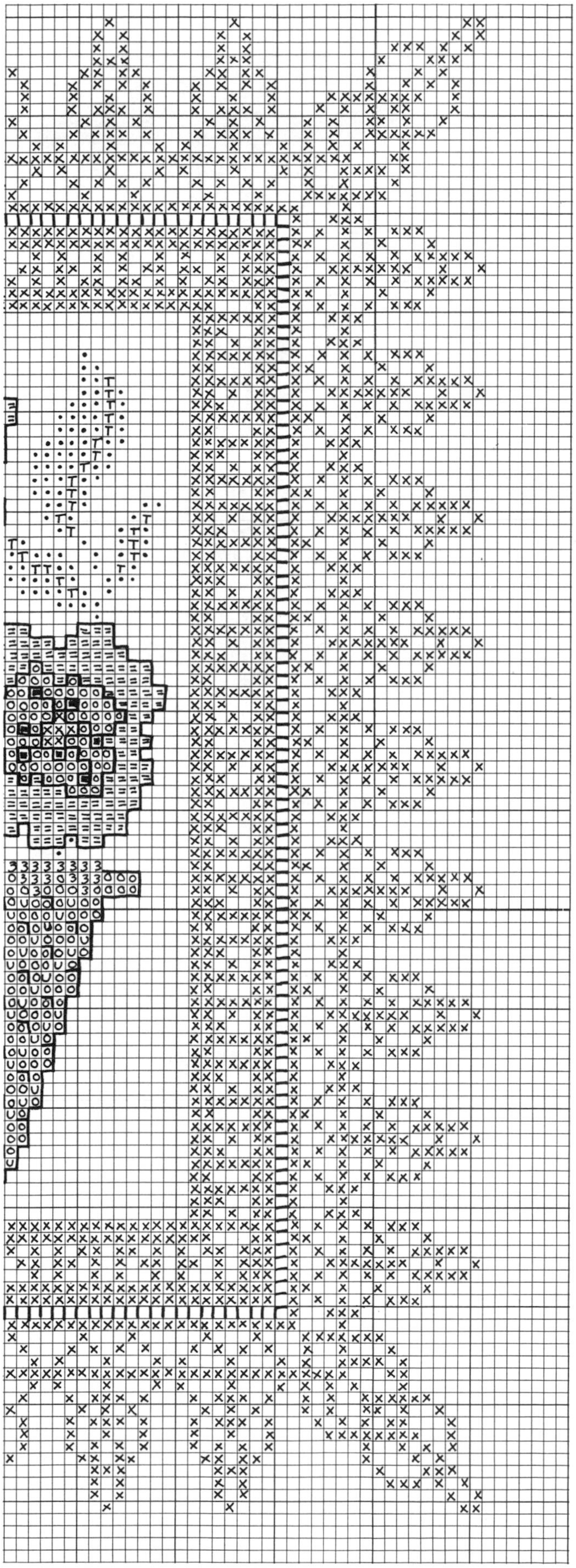

Good Morning, Good Night *(In color, page M, Color Section II)*.

Size: Each embroidery approximately 12¾" wide × 14".

Aida 8, ivory: Cut two fabrics each 33" wide × 25".

Embroidery floss: Coats 6226 Kelly Green (or DMC 702), 1001 White (Snow-White), 2307 Christmas Gold (783), 2302 Orange Lt. (743), 3281 Pink Med. (963), 3001 Cranberry Lt. (957), 3283 Rose (602), 3065 Cranberry Very Dk. (915), 5471 Coffee Brown (433), 6001 Parrot Green Lt. (907), 6228 Christmas Green (909), use DMC color (369), 6020 Nile Green (954), 4101 Violet Dk. (552), 4097 Violet Lt. (554), 3500 Christmas Red (321), 2326 Copper (921), 2327 Pumpkin Bright (970), 7021 Delft (794), 5365 no name (781), 7080 no name (798), 4104 Lavender Dk. (210), 4092 Violet Med. (327), use DMC color (208), use DMC color (828), 5387 Cream (Ecru), 5942 Tan Brown Lt. (437), use DMC color (611), and use DMC color (918). Purchase three skeins each of 6226 Kelly Green (702) and use DMC color (369). Shop for two skeins each of 5471 Coffee Brown (433), 6228 Christmas Green (909), 5365 no name (781), and 5942 Tan Brown Lt. (437). Buy one skein of each remaining color.

Other materials: Medium-weight beige cotton, for back, 1½ yards. Beige pre-gathered eyelet edging, 3½" wide × 5¼ yards. Green grosgrain ribbon, 1" wide × 1 yard. Two standard (26" wide × 20") or queen (30" wide × 20") pillows.

Making the first cross-stitch: On "Good Morning" measure across 12½" from top left corner; measure downwards 5¾" from top left corner. On "Good Night" measure across 15" from top left corner; measure downwards 5¾" from top left corner. Mark point where two measurements intersect. Start sewing at arrow.

Finishing directions

1. "Good Morning" and "Good Night" are exactly the same except for the salutations. Embroider "Good Morning" chart in its entirety. Then embroider "Good Night" and tip of basket handle. Refer again to "Good Morning." Repeat rest of chart.
2. Wash.
3. With right sides up and on each pillow cover, add 13¾" margins on sides and 3⅛" margins at top and bottom. At sides, measure from cross-stitch in center of basket handle. At top, measure from top of "m" and "n". At bottom measure from middle of arch at bottom of basket. Mark with pins. Using knotted single strand of ivory thread, hand-stitch these lines by following one row in Aida and by weaving in and out cloth with 1" running stitches. Check to see that dimensions within these stitches are 27½" wide × 19½" (Illus. 130). These running stitches will later be your markings for matching fabrics and machine-stitching.

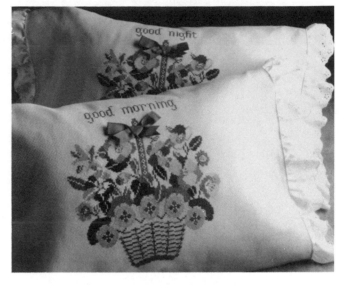

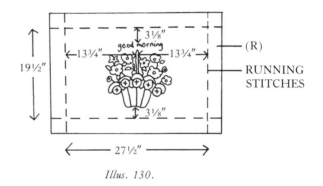

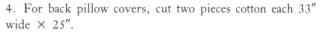

Illus. 130.

4. For back pillow covers, cut two pieces cotton each 33" wide × 25".
5. With right sides together, lay one embroidered front over one back. Pin. Stitch across top on running stitches. Trim seams to ⅝" (Illus. 131); press open. Finish off raw edges at seam with zigzag-stitching.

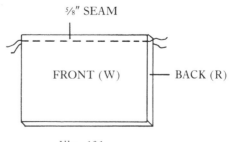

Illus. 131.

6. On each embroidered front, press sides back on running stitches. Press sides back on back cover by using front edges as your pattern. Trim seams to ⅝". Finish off raw edges of fabric with zigzag-stitching (Illus. 132).

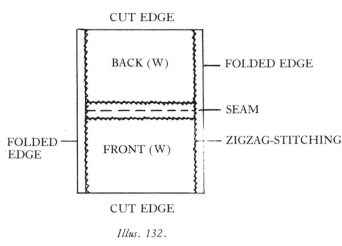

CUT EDGE

BACK (W) — FOLDED EDGE

SEAM

FOLDED
EDGE — FRONT (W) — ZIGZAG-STITCHING

CUT EDGE

Illus. 132.

7. With right sides up, add eyelet edging to sides of pillow covers. Start at top edge of Aida, and baste so that the bottom of the eyelet heading rests under folded edges of sides (Illus. 133).

8. Cut ribbon in half. Make two bows that are 5″ wide, single knotted, and have points cut in ends (Illus. 134). Slip-stitch knot at back of ribbon so bow stays tied.

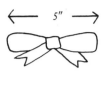

← 5″ →

Illus. 134.

9. With right sides up, place one bow on one embroidered basket. Position bows in center of handles just below first beige triangles. Slip-stitch bows to Aida.

10. With right sides together, stitch across bottom of covers. Sew on running stitches. Trim seam to ⅝″ (Illus. 135); press open. Finish off raw edges at seam with zigzag-stitching.

11. Turn covers. Insert your pillowcase/pillow. If the ends of the pillowcase show, tuck them inwards.

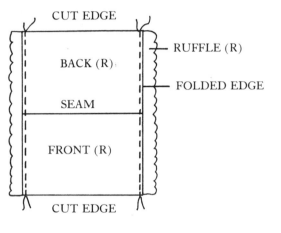

CUT EDGE

— RUFFLE (R)

BACK (R)

— FOLDED EDGE

SEAM

FRONT (R)

CUT EDGE

Illus. 133.

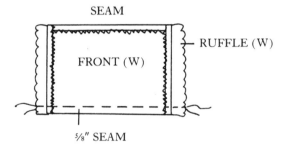

SEAM

FRONT (W) — RUFFLE (W)

⅝″ SEAM

Illus. 135.

Charts and color key on pages 120 and 121.

CROSS-STITCH COLOR KEY

Symbol	J. & P. Coats	DMC
⊠	6226 *Kelly Green*	702
M	1001 *White*	*Snow-White*
■	2307 *Christmas Gold*	783
T	2302 *Orange Lt.*	743
Z	3281 *Pink Med.*	963
Q	3001 *Cranberry Lt.*	957
L	3283 *Rose*	602
S	3065 *Cranberry Very Dk.*	915
V	5471 *Coffee Brown*	433
e	6001 *Parrot Green Lt.*	907
≡	6228 *Christmas Green*	909
·	*Use DMC color*	369
◆	6020 *Nile Green*	954
N	4101 *Violet Dk.*	552
◹	4097 *Violet Lt.*	554
▬	3500 *Christmas Red*	321
C	2326 *Copper*	921
△	2327 *Pumpkin Bright*	970
◻	7021 *Delft*	794
o	5365 *no name*	781
B	7080 *no name*	798
U	4104 *Lavender Dk.*	210
K	4092 *Violet Med.*	327
H	*Use DMC color*	208
◨	*Use DMC color*	828
◿	5387 *Cream*	*Ecru*
3	5942 *Tan Brown Lt.*	437
A	*Use DMC color*	611
♥	*Use DMC color*	918
◻	*Fabric as is*	

BACKSTITCH COLOR KEY

Symbol	Area	J. & P. Coats	DMC
	Center of all flowers; outline around one pink flower and bud.	5471 *Coffee Brown*	433

Teakettle and Fruit *(In color, page N, Color Section II)*.

Size: Wall hanging approximately 13⅞″ wide × 12⅞″.

Cork linen, 19-thread count, bleached: Cut fabric 18″ wide × 17″.

Embroidery floss: Coats 5365 no name (435), 5472 Coffee Brown Med. (898), 5471 Coffee Brown (801), 6256 Parrot Green Med. (3347), 2099 Pumpkin (740), 2335 Nasturtium (350), 2293 Yellow Dark (use Coats color), 6267 Avocado Green (469), 6001 Parrot Green Lt. (907), 2292 Golden Yellow Very Lt. (3078), use DMC color (472), use DMC color (210), use DMC color (208), use DMC color (833), 2332 Burnt Orange Dk. (900), 2327 Pumpkin Bright (970), use DMC color (402), use DMC color (919), use DMC color (830), 2302 Orange Lt. (743), 2326 Copper (920), 1001 White (Snow-White), 3151 Cranberry Very Lt. (3326), 3153 Geranium (956), use DMC color (761), use DMC color (729), 3281 Pink Med. (963), 7010 Imperial Blue (use Coats color), and 7021 Delft (809). Purchase three skeins of each of use DMC color (210) and use DMC color (761). Shop for two skeins of 3281 Pink Med. (963). Buy one skein of each remaining color.

Making the first cross-stitch: Measure across 3″ from top left corner; measure downwards 3″ from top left corner. Mark point where two measurements intersect. Start sewing at arrow.

Finishing directions

1. See "Mounting and Framing."
2. Margin to be added at mounting: Add 1″.

CROSS-STITCH COLOR KEY

Symbol	J. & P. Coats	DMC
⊡	5365 no name	435
◥	5472 Coffee Brown Med.	898
◆	5471 Coffee Brown	801
M	6256 Parrot Green Med.	3347
Z	2099 Pumpkin	740
▲	2335 Nasturtium	350
=	2293 Yellow Dark	Use J. & P. Coats color
e	6267 Avocado Green	469
△	6001 Parrot Green Lt.	907
♥	2292 Golden Yellow Very Lt.	3078
C	Use DMC color	472
⊠	Use DMC color	210
◢	Use DMC color	208
⋻	Use DMC color	833
⊠	2332 Burnt Orange Dk.	900

Symbol	J. & P. Coats	DMC
∨	2327 Pumpkin Bright	970
⊍	Use DMC color	402
T	Use DMC color	919
N	Use DMC color	830
S	2302 Orange Lt.	743
∕	2326 Copper	920
L	1001 White	Snow-White
■	3151 Cranberry Very Lt.	3326
K	3153 Geranium	956
·	Use DMC color	761
◨	Use DMC color	729
■	3281 Pink Med.	963
◰	7010 Imperial Blue	Use J. & P. Coats color
⊓	7021 Delft	809
☐	Fabric as is	

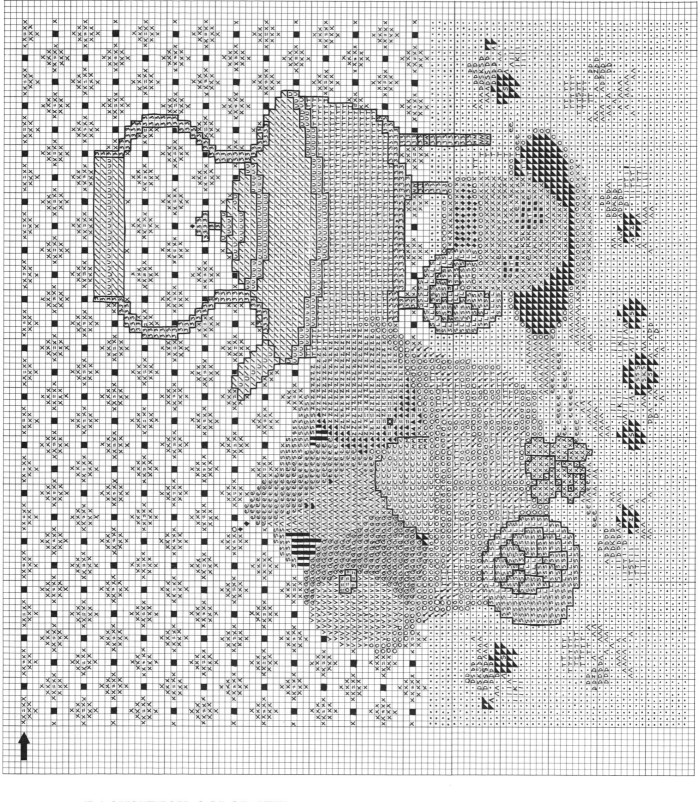

BACKSTITCH COLOR KEY

Symbol	Area	J. & P. Coats	DMC
	All.	*5471 Coffee Brown*	*801*

MOUNTING
AND FRAMING

Materials and Techniques

White Mat Board.
100% Polyester Batting.
Bleached Muslin.
One-inch Masking Tape.
White Six-strand Cotton Floss.
Regular Sewing Thread.
Ruler.
Mat Knife.
Pliers.
Large Crewel Needle.
Straight Pins.

In the few projects that require mounting and framing, there is a heading entitled "Margin to be added at mounting." It is here that you are asked to add a specified margin (¾" to 1½") to all four sides of the design before the mounting procedure can begin. These additional inches, which butt into the seam allowances, give a breather between the edge of the embroidery and the edge of the frame. To mount, for example, "Teakettle and Fruit" (1" margins required), follow this basic routine:

1. On one side of artwork, locate the very edge of design. Measure 1" (this number changes) beyond this point; mark spot with pin. On three remaining sides of picture, mark 1" margins. Measure from edge of design. Pin.

2. With knotted single strand of thread, connect these four points. To do so, hand-stitch these lines by following one row in fabric and by weaving in and out cloth with large running stitches. These stitched lines are now the edges of your needlework.

3. Measure length and width of newly stitched shape (Illus. 136).

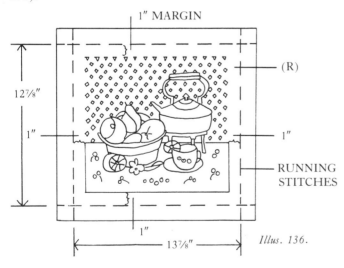

Illus. 136.

4. Cut three pieces of mat board, each measuring dimensions in Step 3. Stack them together; tape in north-south-east-west position (Illus. 137).

5. Cut one piece polyester batting measuring dimensions in Step 3. Lay batting over boards.

6. Cut one piece muslin; add 2" seam allowance to all sides of dimensions in Step 3. With right sides up, center muslin over batting/mat board combination. On back, fold in top and bottom. Tape. Fold in sides. Tape temporarily (Illus. 138).

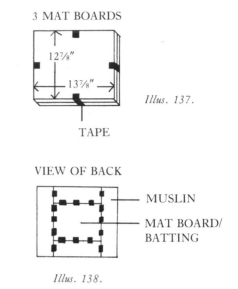

Illus. 137.

7. With right sides down, lay embroidery flat; lay muslin/batting/mat board combination on top and within stitched edges of design. Fold in top and bottom. Tape. Fold in sides. Tape. Get corners neat and flat.

8. On back of design, sew four corners flat with ½" running stitches. Use crewel needle and six-strand cotton floss. If necessary, use pliers to pull needle through.

9. While still on back of design, lace back and forth between finished-off edges of top and bottom. To do, start at one side and work towards other. Cut floss into 2 yard lengths. Insert needle ³⁄₁₆" beyond folded and stitched edges of cloth (Illus. 139). As you approach end of each thread,

Illus. 139.

Illus. 140.

check to see that edge of design line rests on edge of mat board. Check also to see that needlework is centered, flat, and slightly taut.

10. Lace in opposite direction and in same manner (Illus. 140).

11. Remove edge of design threads and any tape.

12. Add frame. Glass is not necessary.

Metric Equivalents

INCHES TO MILLIMETRES AND CENTIMETRES

MM—millimetres   *CM—centimetres*

Inches	MM	CM	Inches	CM	Inches	CM
⅛	3	0.3	9	22.9	30	76.2
¼	6	0.6	10	25.4	31	78.7
⅜	10	1.0	11	27.9	32	81.3
½	13	1.3	12	30.5	33	83.8
⅝	16	1.6	13	33.0	34	86.4
¾	19	1.9	14	35.6	35	88.9
⅞	22	2.2	15	38.1	36	91.4
1	25	2.5	16	40.6	37	94.0
1¼	32	3.2	17	43.2	38	96.5
1½	38	3.8	18	45.7	39	99.1
1¾	44	4.4	19	48.3	40	101.6
2	51	5.1	20	50.8	41	104.1
2½	64	6.4	21	53.3	42	106.7
2	76	7.6	22	55.9	43	109.2
3½	89	8.9	23	58.4	44	111.8
4	102	10.2	24	61.0	45	114.3
4½	114	11.4	25	63.5	46	116.8
5	127	12.7	26	66.0	47	119.4
6	152	15.2	27	68.6	48	121.9
7	178	17.8	28	71.1	49	124.5
8	203	20.3	29	73.7	50	127.0

INDEX